A Capital Place

A Capital Place

✦

Reminiscences of a Sandy Lake Boyhood

By David Laursen

Writers Club Press
New York Lincoln Shanghai

A Capital Place
Reminiscences of a Sandy Lake Boyhood

Writers Club Press
an imprint of iUniverse, Inc.

For information address:
iUniverse, Inc.
2021 Pine Lake Road, Suite 100
Lincoln, NE 68512
www.iuniverse.com

ISBN: 0-595-22529-2

Printed in the United States of America

Contents

PROLOGUE 1

CHAPTER 1   BEGINNING AT THE END OF THE
              ROAD 3

CHAPTER 2   EARLIEST IMPRESSIONS 25

CHAPTER 3   THE SUMMER PEOPLE 49

CHAPTER 4   THE SUMMER OF '46 63

CHAPTER 5   COMING OF THE HIGHWAY 81

CHAPTER 6   RICHARD THE LIONHEART 95

CHAPTER 7   OLD JIM 107

CHAPTER 8   THE LUCK OF THE IRISH 125

CHAPTER 9   CONFESSIONS OF A CONFIRMED
              RICE BEATER 141

CHAPTER 10   THE LINCOLN AND THE CADILLAC 159

CHAPTER 11   FRIENDS AND FOLLIES OF A
              FRESHMAN 175

CHAPTER 12   SOPHOMORE HI-JINKS 189

CHAPTER 13   A STUDENT'S SEARCH FOR
              MEANING 199

CHAPTER 14   WEDDING BELLS 205

PROLOGUE

Sandy Lake—the "Capital Place" referred to in the title of this story—was once the capital of the Ojibwe Nation. Before that, it was an ancestral home of the Sioux and even earlier tribes dating back thousands of years. The history of these early peoples—who hunted mastodons in the shadows of the glaciers—is obviously lost in antiquity.

I find it just as interesting to speculate on the origins of the land itself—that far-off time when brown bedrock first emerged from the womb of the melting glacier like the head of a babe from the birth canal. The infant landscape, gouged and bruised by unimaginable pressures, must have resembled a carelessly plowed field, pocked with craters and lonely boulders strewn about haphazardly as though the devil had been on a drunken spree. Or perhaps God Himself had done the plowing.

As the ice retreated, my future home on Sandy Lake gradually rose on the northern shore of Glacial Lake Aitkin—the result perhaps of sand and gravels carried down from the north and deposited here by glacial rivers. With Glacial Lake Agassiz to the west, and predawn Lake Superior to the east, the rising hills surrounding Sandy Lake must have remained an island in a watery sea for a very long time. What did the Sandy Lake country look like the day God finished his plowing and walked away? Imagine seeing it through a time-delay camera, the land newly sculptured—all sharp edges and jagged slopes with rocks and vast hunks of ice dotting the landscape, and then these same slopes rounded by rain and taking on a green tint as grass and mosses began to root in the barren soil. And then imagine a tall grass prairie of wild flowers waving in the summer breeze, and woody shrubs creeping up the sheltered gullies. How much wind did it take and how much rain to smooth these rugged hills and valleys into their present configuration? When did the first squirrel carry the first acorn up from the south and plant the first oak?

And think of the lake itself, a mound of dirt covering massive blocks of ice that had broken off from the glacier proper. How long did it take for these blocks of ice to melt, creating Bell Horn Bay, Glacier Lake, and other deep lakes in the area—lakes silt-laden and no better than gravel pits? How many centuries before these waters turned clear and capable of supporting fish migrating up unknown waterways. And finally, we see the wonderful bounty of the harvest: the oaks, the wild rice beds, the sugar maple trees, the thundering wings of a billion waterfowl as Glacial Lake Aitkin becomes a shallow marsh. The stage was now set, the seeds planted for those future wars of possession which continued for the next few thousand years. Sandy Lake became the temporary home of a succession of peoples: unknown aborigines, the moundbuilders, the Sioux, the Ojibwe, the French, the British, the Americans, the trapper, the logger, the farmer, and finally the sportsmen—men and women who do for amusement what the native people did for survival. These latter day nimrods needed a warm meal and a place to get out of the rain. My father, sometime around 1934, decided to provide these amenities. To my knowledge he never regretted that decision or ever looked back. The pages that follow are all about looking back.

1

BEGINNING AT THE END OF THE ROAD

There is no place quite so exciting for a boy to grow up as the end of the road. The world, though it may touch you there, cannot quite corner you, and many of our neighbors undoubtedly moved to the end of the road for that reason. Most of these people had nothing to hide perhaps, but were simply cast off quite accidentally from the main stream and deposited like logs at the high water mark in this northern backwater. Like grounded logs, they lacked the means or impetus to leave, and gradually fell into ruin.

Others had come for quite different reasons. These were the returning veterans of the Great War, who had been wrenched from their homes as boys and transplanted to the trenches of France, where they were watered with rain and blood and fertilized with the droppings of rats and the putrefying flesh of their comrades. They left home the rankest of country bumpkins, and those that survived returned wounded in spirit if not in body, with wise and cynical eyes, to whom life in the backwater looked good indeed.

Some of these returnees had been exposed to mustard gas and were drawing small veterans pensions. I never noticed that these pensioners looked particularly sickly. Indeed, they all appeared to be strong and vigorous men, tireless on their traplines, and capable of walking untold generations of white-tailed deer into the ground. Their latent ill health only manifested itself at the prospect—or even the suggestion—of steady work.

No country hicks these men. At the time I took it for granted, but looking back now I marvel at the overall intelligence and competence of these people. Most read books and newspapers and never missed the noontime news on WCCO, the only station with a strong-enough signal to reach our northern home. They were curious and well informed. The end of the road, I decided—at least in those years—did not attract fools but the opposite: the free spirit, the bold, the capable. They had learned during the war that their government could neither be depended upon, or trusted, and that long-term prospects were quite up to them.

The world currents that had brought our neighbors to Sandy Lake had brought my father farthest of all—from the tiny island of Fyn in the country of Denmark. After a 15-year stopover in Austin, Minnesota, where he learned to speak English, saved his money, and took a young bride, he arrived at Sandy Lake in 1934 with his ideals intact, a capitalistic streak, and a puritan work ethic—qualities that did not necessarily endear him to his more cynical neighbors. My father's goal in coming to the United States, like many immigrants, was to strike it rich. The goal of many of our neighbors was simply to remain on strike. These differing life viewpoints naturally created some mutual suspicion and even contempt, though these people were probably more alike than they knew.

They were each being rebels in their own way. My father had fled the rule of kings, rebelling against a rigid class system that discouraged initiative and prevented one from getting ahead. In the new world, initiative was encouraged and expected, which I suppose is why some of our neighbors rebelled against that notion. Being independent people, you can almost predict that each would swim in their own way against the prevailing tides.

There is something to be said for both viewpoints. Our veterans of the Great War, as innocent youth, had barely escaped with their lives, teaching them that life—their own in particular—was the only riches of value. To live each day as though it were your last, savoring the beauty around you, with as little effort or discomfort as possible—that may have seemed to be the only sensible way to live. At this period in history, at the end of the road, such a life was even quite possible. If our wounded veterans missed the booming twenties they missed the bust of the thirties also. During the depression the country was the right place for the unemployed to be. The surrounding wilderness, or a small clearing in the forest, could provide food and fuel, and even a cash crop in the way of fur or timber. The depression years were really the heyday of this country. Every clearing of 40 acres or more held a family, and every smaller plot a recluse.

Families could survive and even prosper here, mainly because they could escape the cash economy altogether. They had no house payment, no utility bills, no telephones, no insurance, no car payments, no indoor plumbing. Many of them were 20th century disciples of Thoreau, without ever knowing his name.

There were also some genuine farmers in the area, homesteaders or the descendents of homesteaders, who were determined to wring a living from the poorly drained bottom lands along the Mississippi River, or in the bogs south of Sandy Lake where occasional patches of ground rose high enough above the bog for a field to be established and a house built. A few thousand years earlier these higher areas had been islands in Glacial Lake Aitkin. Now the great lake was gone, but its evolution into dry ground was not yet complete. Beneath the bogs of peat laid down by centuries of decaying vegetation, the waters of Glacial Lake Aitkin still lurked to seize the feet and the automobiles of the unwary. Indomitable homesteaders, many of Finnish descent, eventually succeeded in establishing productive dairy farms on this forbidding ground, raised large families, and became pillars of the community.

But these homesteaders and their farms were mostly to the south of Sandy Lake, or several miles north along the Mississippi River, and were not our close neighbors. Sandy Lake was where the forest began, the land lifting out of the bog into rolling hills of pine and hardwoods, and in the valleys between the hills were numerous lakes left behind by the retreating glacier. From the look of this land the glacier must have rested here for some time before retreating north. Its unimaginable weight depressed the land and dredged the craters which have since filled with water to become Sandy Lake, Minnewawa, Glacier Lake, and others in the area.

Beneath the glacier were underground streams which deposited sand and gravel from the melting ice to form those long and narrow ridges which we call eskers. Many of these eskers run north and south, indicating the southward flow of streams into Glacial Lake Aitkin. Conifers found these gravelly ridges fertile ground, and today many still bear fine stands of red and white pine, spruce, and balsam fir.

Glacial Lake Aitkin itself drained south, hitting the bed of the present Mississippi River somewhere between the towns of Aitkin and Brainerd. The youthful river cut a narrow gorge through bedrock in the Brainerd area, indicating that the river spilling out of Glacial Lake Aitkin was swift, but not particularly wide. (See Folwells History of Minnesota, Vol I). Today, north of Aitkin, the Mississippi River wanders in great loops across the ancient lake bottom, the river bed not sufficiently deep to drain the bottomlands completely, allowing the ancient lake to partially resurrect itself during wet springs or periods of heavy rainfall. Today, instead of draining directly south, the vast bog that was once Lake Aitkin now drains north through Sandy Lake, and through the locks of the Corp of Engineers dam which sits astride the lake's Sandy River outlet. Less than a mile downstream from the dam, the Sandy River joins the Mississippi on its 2000 mile journey to the Gulf of Mexico.

It was the strategic significance of these waterways in ancient times which led directly to the colorful and often bloody history of this area into which I was dropped so fortuitously as a babe in 1935 without being asked and quite possibly against my will.

◆　　　◆　　　◆

My parents arrived at Sandy Lake a year before I was born and took up residence in a store purchased from a man named McKay. Along with the store went four small rental cabins, a dock, and four or five flat-bottom wooden boats whose bottoms needed a layer of tar every year to keep them afloat. The store came equipped with a post office, and—because there was a post office—the site of the store was listed on official highway maps as a town—the name of the town being Libby.

Libby, it seems, had been a real person who had come to the area as a young man to try the fishing. He failed to return home. His parents, alarmed, sent another son in search of the first and the second son never returned either. The story does not relate whether the Libby family ran out of children to send, or whether they did not wish to risk another on a journey to Sandy Lake. Or perhaps they came looking themselves. At any rate, when the Libby boys saw the pine forests surrounding Sandy Lake they saw their future and the future looked good. In time, they became noted lumbermen in the area. When the pine forests were depleted, I suspect the Libby boys skedadled west with the Weyerhausers and other lumber barons. The reason I suspect this is that our mail was occasionally misrouted to a place called Libby, Montana—perhaps another place where the Libby boys had stopped long enough on their way west to name a town.

Because of the Libby post office, my father had thus bought himself a town as well as a store, and became the unappointed town postmaster, a job which paid little, but possibly kept us from starving during the depression years when money was almost non-existent.

At one time Libby had been a real town located a half-mile to the north on a peninsula between the Sandy and Mississippi Rivers. Here, where the rivers joined, was a rock pier where steamboats docked, and the houses of Libby stood in a row along the river bank on a spit of land so narrow that you could dive off your porch into either the

Sandy River, or the Mississippi, depending on whether you dove east or west.

The town was ideally located for steamboat traffic, but once the big boats stopped running there was no advantage to a town being jammed between two rivers—quite a disadvantage really—so the town was moved, perhaps board by board, or it may have simply rotted away. At any rate, when I was a boy, only a few holes in the ground marked the remains of this once thriving village, which—like some fickle lover—had abandoned the river to run off to the nearest road which had pushed its way to the north end of Sandy Lake a half mile to the south.

Or perhaps it was just the Libby post office that had moved south, ending up by chance in Mr. McKay's store, where it spawned a new town with the old name. A post office, I decided, is as free to move as the old Ark of the Covenant, and takes with it all its authority, power, and trappings of officialdom, regardless of where it resides.

The site where McKay decided to build his store and resort on the northwest end of Sandy Lake was ideally situated, and indeed—had been a town site for hundreds if not thousands of years. Here, between two wooded points, the Sandy River had once flowed through a grassy meadow as it left Sandy Lake on its short journey to the Mississippi. On the west side of the river where it left the lake was a point of high ground upon which stood the wigwams of countless generations of the aborigines—some of whom we know but most lost in antiquity. Suffice it to say that here, on this scenic south-facing point, thousands of native Americans caught the sunrise and the rising moon sparkling across the big water to the south. For hundreds of years the real life descendents of Hiawatha had fought and died for this particular piece of lakeshore overlooking Sandy Lake.

The reason was simple. Whoever controlled this piece of real estate controlled canoe travel from both east and west and from north and south. The village site was on the only water route between Lake Superior and the Mississippi River in northern Minnesota. No canoe could pass on its way from Lake Superior without being seen by the villagers. Likewise, the village was near enough to the Mississippi to monitor canoe traffic passing north or south on that great river. Sandy Lake was thus northern Minnesota's equivalent of the straits of Gibraltor, or the pass at Thermopolye. Nobody could proceed beyond this point except at the pleasure (or over the dead bodies) of the Sandy Lake villagers. Both methods were repeatedly attempted. And it was a prize worth fighting for. The tribe that controlled Sandy Lake and the Mississippi River held dominion over a vast portion of northern Minnesota with all its natural resources—the wild rice beds, the maple groves, and the hunting and fishing grounds of Leech Lake, Winnebegoshes, Bowstring, Gull, and other lakes and streams too numerous to mention.

When the French fur trader Sieur du Luth passed this way in the early 1600s' Sandy Lake was Sioux country and had been for perhaps a hundred years. The Sioux had driven out the country's previous occupants, but already their own days were numbered. Du luth had been buying furs from the Ojibwe who were now occupying the shores of Lake Superior after having been driven from their own ancestral homes in the east. Ojibwe guides undoubtedly accompanied Du Luth on his visit to Sandy Lake. What thoughts of future conquest must have occupied the guides' thoughts as their eyes took in the beauty and bounty of this wonderful country?

At any rate, the Ojibwe were not long in returning to Sandy Lake armed with guns obtained from their close association and intermarriage with the French. The Sandy Lake Sioux were still in a stone age culture and no match for the invading Ojibwe armed with French firearms. The Ojibwe well knew that Sandy lake was the key to controlling the upper Mississippi. The sand beaches of Sandy Lake thus took on the nature of a Normandy invasion. Spectacular battles were fought here, including one of the only known naval battles to be fought in Minnesota between Indians from canoes near the site of a small island appropriately named Battle Island.

One morning, while still in my teens, I sat on the shore of Battle Island watching a spread of duck decoys, hoping without success to attract a raft of mallards sitting on the big water to the east. It was an overcast, somewhat foggy morning without a breath of wind, and quite warm for October. I sat enclosed by the fog and my own daydreams, listening to the mallards talking to each other on the big water in perfect safety, the sound of their voices carrying so perfectly in the stillness that it seemed as though I were sitting in their midst. As I sat on the high-water line of the beach I carefully picked through a layer of small stones deposited high and dry by the waves, or by the ice, and soon found what I was looking for. What I found was a perfect flint scraper crafted by some aborigine who predated both the Ojibwe and the Sioux. It was an exquisite piece of work, perhaps two inches square, quite flat, with each side terminating in a point with a curving half-moon between the points. I had no idea what it might have been used for, but I marveled at the workmanship—how the rock had been precisely formed, one chip at a time.

I pocketed this treasure, eager to look for more, but then my friends came and took me away. Battle Island was several miles away from my home and I never returned. But many times I have dreamed of the treasures buried there in the sand, and of that morning in the foggy silence when the ghosts of the Indian people were all around me, and my intuition was alive with possibility.

By this time, of course, I was aware that my home was built practically on the ruins of ancient Indian civilizations, and I had been picking up artifacts for years, mostly pieces of broken pottery—not in any organized way but simply by walking the beaches to see what the waves had exposed.

This beach I walked had not always been a beach. Before the Sandy Lake dam raised the level of the lake by several feet, this had been an original home site of countless generations of aborigines. Now the beach was a magic tablet, rewritten each day by the waves and shifting water levels. Water levels are capricious by nature, but never more so than now when the water levels are controlled by the Corp of Engineers, an authority sometimes higher and more capricious than God.

As the lake levels were lowered each fall to accommodate the spring snow-melt, the old village site gradually rose above the surface like some sunken Atlantis. Crashing waves marched down its watery streets, sifting through the sands of this ancient village to expose the detritus of centuries: pottery, scrapers, an occasional arrowhead, even a peace pipe perhaps fashioned in more modern times by the Sioux. However, most of the year the old village site remained beneath the waves, and one could walk on its shallow grave almost to the middle of our bay, until—if you continued on—you fell into the sudden drop-off marking the old riverbed which still flowed beneath its waters.

Who were these people who had dwelled for centuries on the beach where I now swam on sunny summer afternoons? The Sioux and the Ojibwe we know about, because they lived here during the period of European occupation. But who came before? There is good evidence that the Sioux had conquered this land and driven out its previous owners quite recently, perhaps no more than a hundred years before Du Luth's visit to Sandy Lake in the early 1600's.

The Ojibwe historian Warren relates how a Red Lake Ojibwe, visiting the remnant of a once powerful tribe along the Missouri River, was shown a piece of birch bark upon which was depicted a perfectly accurate map of Sandy Lake and its tributaries. The map's possessor, an old man, told the Red Lake Ojibwe that Sandy Lake had once been the ancestral home of his people. Now this once proud tribe had been so decimated by war and disease that other tribes took pity upon them and allowed its remaining few to dwell in peace along the Missouri. Here then was another tribe who had yielded up their Sandy Lake home, and was about to give up existence itself.

But this dying tribe may itself have conquered and evicted the land's previous occupants—a group known as mound builders due to the distinctive shape of their dwellings which suggest that they may have lived at least partially underground. The mound builders must have been numerous indeed, for their mounds are found all across Minnesota, including Sandy Lake. The historian Warren reports that such mounds were common along the Prairie River, the old canoe route between Lake Superior and Sandy Lake. Now the mound areas have been over-taken by forests, but I have personally stumbled upon them in my travels through the lake country.

Some historians believe that the mounds were burial grounds rather than living quarters because human bones have been found within the mounds. However, the Indian elders who Warren interviewed believed that the bones resulted from the inhabitants being slaughtered in their dwellings and left there. As evidence, the elders cited hatchet marks and other trauma to the bones which would be inconsistent with nor-mal burial. Of course, it is equally possible that the buried victims were killed in battle, and then buried. Nobody knows. Nor can anyone explain why the mound builders disappeared.

◆   ◆   ◆

Growing up as a boy nobody had to tell me that I was living in a special place. But it was not until later that it occurred to me that my family and I were among a long line of usurpers who had found this land fair and had taken it—either by strength of arms or through the power of the law which rules that land can be bought and sold by the last person or entity to claim it. The last entity, in this case, was the United States government, who took it from the British, who took it from the French, who never owned it either. There is an old saying that possession is nine/tenths of law, and—in the case of land—posses-sion is everything. Unoccupied land (aborigines do not count) is con-sidered a natural treasure, like gold or diamonds, and free for the taking by those who are first to find it, or strong enough to keep it afterwards. And like any treasure, it forms the basis of future war.

There was no shortage of war on this plot of lakeshore which my father had purchased from Mr. McKay in 1934. How privileged I was to be allowed to grow up in peace here, on a hill overlooking the watery grave of a village for whose possession countless races of redmen had fought and died. The two most recent combatants—the Sioux and the Ojibwe—were not simply cousins who had had a falling out. They were strangers, dissimilar in stature, their root languages totally different; they might have come from opposite sides of the moon. But it was not their differences but territory at the root of their battles.

The Ojibwe had been evicted from their ancestral homes in the east and needed to find another to hold their burgeoning population. They had already swept down both shores of Lake Superior, driving out the Fox and other tribes as they went. For many years their capital city was on Madeline Island in Lake Superior, a place easy to defend while they increased in strength and numbers. Now they were about to stake their claim to the northern Minnesota Lake country by way of Sandy Lake.

It is easy to understand why the Ojibwe coveted Sandy Lake. Not only did it have strategic location, but it abounded in riches of the edible kind. The Sandy River which flowed in front of the village and my future home was alive each spring with spawning fish moving upstream from the Mississippi River into Sandy Lake. In my mind's eye I can see the water churning with great schools of walleyes and northern pike moving upriver just after the ice went out, followed by redhorse and giant buffalo fish weighing up to 30 pounds—a veritable feast swimming practically into the village. I can see children standing on the riverbank with makeshift spears, and whitefish drying on racks in the sun.

The hills surrounding Sandy Lake were covered with sugar maple trees, and each spring there were pots boiling throughout the sugar bush as the woman made maple sugar while the men were off spearing muskrats in the shallow backwaters which bordered the Sandy and Prairie Rivers. These backwaters were a treasure trove year around—supporting not only thousands of muskrat houses, but great stands of wild rice, which was probably the most important and reliable food in the Indian diet. In the shallow wild rice beds, ducks, geese and other shorebirds nested by the thousands, and undoubtedly gathered there in the fall by the hundreds of thousands.

This was indeed a land of milk and honey, as well as a place of great beauty. Lovely wooded points provided acorns and shelter from the winds. Directly to the south of the old village were islands of various sizes, all with curving sand beaches where shiner minnows came up in the shallows after dark, with great schools of walleyes following. As a boy my father and I spent many summer evenings along these beaches seining minnows, and I can remember the feel of large fish bumping into our small seine attempting to escape. Sometimes they would bump my bare leg on their way out, provoking a startled gasp in the darkness. They might be large pike with sharp teeth, or monsters of the deep, depending on where your imagination led.

Night after night I would help drag the seine through the water in the dark, stumbling over sunken logs or slippery rocks, my father in deep water to the height of his waders, me on the shallow end, tugging the seine along by means of a five-foot wooden stick to which the seine was tied, careful to keep the weighted edge of the seine on the sand bottom so as to prevent the captured minnows from slipping under the seine. When father decided we had traveled far enough through the water we would drag the seine ashore and look for the silvery, wiggling treasure therein. Sometimes, after all this effort, we would find only two or three minnows in the seine. One night on a rocky shore where we had never seined before, we caught a thousand shiners in a single haul. This was treasure indeed, because shiner minnows were difficult to obtain during the summer and even harder to keep alive. These would not live long either, but long enough to give our fishermen guests happy faces in the morning.

In this way I gained an appreciation for the bounty of this land which nevertheless was already disappearing by the time I was growing up.

But this bounty was here in abundance when the Ojibwe invaded the Sioux village on Sandy Lake sometime during the 1700's and ultimately prevailed in battle. Sandy Lake thus became an Ojibwe village, and ultimately replaced La Pointe on Madeline Island as the capital of the Ojibwe nation.

But the battle for Sandy Lake was far from over. Eventually the Sioux too obtained firearms, and the battle odds became more even. For the next hundred years a bloody war raged up and down the Mississippi River, as well as east and west from Lake Superior to the Red River. Neither man, woman, or child were safe from marauding bands anywhere in the lake country. For more than a century this became the "dark and bloody" ground where no Indian family traveled except with "fear and trembling."

The Sioux were unable to dislodge the Ojibwe from Sandy Lake partly because new Ojibwe immigrants kept arriving from villages on Lake Superior faster than the Sioux could kill them off. Eventually the Sioux were expelled from their villages all across the northern lake country, and eventually took up residence on the Rum River near present Elk River and also along the Minnesota River. From these locations they continued to wage war on the Ojibwe for a century. According to Sioux elders, the Mississippi River current gave the Ojibwe an advantage during the tribes' periodic attacks on each other's villages. The Ojibwe, from their base on Sandy Lake, could drift downstream in well provisioned canoes to attack the Sioux, while the Sioux had to paddle their way upstream fighting a powerful current, or walk, and were exhausted and sometimes starving by the time they reached Sandy Lake.

Nevertheless, the Sioux were successful enough in this bloody game of tit for tat, until they made the fatal mistake of attacking white settlers in 1862 and were banished from the state by white soldiers. The Ojibwe, perhaps because of their long association and intermarriage with French fur traders, were careful to avoid killing whites, and the few times it happened they themselves turned over the murderer to face white justice. When asked to assist the British in fighting Americans during the war of 1812, Flat Mouth, the Leech Lake Ojibwe chieftain, remarked that he would never interfere in a white man's battles, nor would he so much as break a window in a white man's dwelling.

But it was not just the Sioux who created havoc among the Ojibwe conquerors of Sandy Lake. In 1782 an Ojibwe traveler returning from Lake Superior brought smallpox—the "red death"—to the Sandy Lake village. So many died that Warren, the Ojibwe historian, wrote that the entire village—once the proud capital of the Ojibwe nation—was reduced to seven wigwams.

By the time the Northwest Company established their fur trading post on Sandy Lake in 1793, the population of the Sandy Lake village had largely recovered its numbers through immigrants from Lake Superior. Then, in 1800, disaster struck the Sandy Lake tribe once again. That spring, while returning from an extended hunt along the Crow Wing River to the west, the Sandy Lake band was overtaken by a Sioux war party on Cross Lake and nearly annihilated. The only people to escape were a few Sandy Lake women who had gone on ahead to establish the next evening's campsite. The only other survivor was a young girl, who—when the battle started, saved herself by hiding in a pine tree. But once again, the Sandy Lake village recovered from this tragedy and continued to raise up important war chiefs for the next 50 years.

Little did I know as a boy growing up that the lovely and peaceful vista that greeted me each morning from my bedroom window had long been a scene of strife and terror. The old village that had once stood on my very doorstep was gone now without a trace, submerged beneath risen waters. The famous Northwest Company fort and trading post which had dominated a wooded point a mile down the shore from my home was also gone, not a log remaining, not even an indentation to mark its grave.

Yet this had been a busy and important place once. The great explorer, Zebulon Pike, had found it so when he stumbled hungry and half frozen into the Sandy Lake post in January of 1805 on his search for the source of the Mississippi River. Pike had come by way of the river all the way from St Louis and had been caught in the freeze-up. He pushed on from Little Falls, over the treacherous river ice, and had suffered one disaster after another. His tent burned down. His gear broke through the ice, and he lost his leggings, moccasins and stockings, though he saved his gunpowder which happened to be in watertight containers. I suspect he might have preferred to have rescued his stockings.

Pike pushed on with a companion and arrived at the Sandy Lake post after dark, no doubt ecstatic at finding civilization and a warm meal. Pike reports in his diary, *Expeditions*, that he found the Northwest Company employees living in comfort, dining on Irish potatoes which they grew themselves on a four-acre plot outside the stockade. They also kept horses at the fort, and had an abundance of fish and game in most seasons. Their basic staple, however, was the "wild oats" (wild rice) which they purchased from the Indians at $1.50 a bushel—a pittance considering that the annual wild rice harvest was as critical to the Indian way of life as flooding of the Nile to the ancient Egyptians. When the wild rice crop failed, as it sometimes did due to storms or summer flooding, it was a hungry winter indeed.

What did Pike see that winter evening as he stumbled past my future doorstep in search of the Northwest Company post a full mile to the south ? Was it a night of full moon where he could see the gloomy outline of the fort across the bay? Was there smoke rising from the post chimney? A flickering candle? Did the Sandy Lake Ojibwe villagers, whose encampment he must first pass, show him the way? Did their dogs bark at the approach of this unexpected (and possibly very dangerous) intruder? After all, this stranger might be with a Sioux war party. How did Pike identify himself when he reached the village to avoid being shot by accident?

After a few days rest at the Sandy Lake post, Pike and his men continued on their quest for the source of the Mississippi River. They thought they had found it when they reached Cass Lake, at which point they turned around and began their long and difficult trek back to St Louis. It would be another 15 years before the Mississippi's true source at Lake Itasca was finally discovered by another group of explorers under the direction of Lewis Cass.

Zebulon Pike was not the last famous explorer to enjoy the hospitality of the Sandy Lake post. Indeed, situated as it was on what is now known as Brown's Point, the fort would have been almost impossible to miss. Any traveler from Lake Superior would pass within a half-mile of the stockade gates. Likewise, the post was near enough to the Mississippi River that any visitor making the half-mile journey from the river to Sandy Lake would spot the post immediately upon entering Sandy Lake.

Little did I know as I looked across the lake towards Browns Point what illustrious guests had once stayed in that vanished trading post. The guest list would read like a "who's who" of Minnesota history. Perhaps half of northern Minnesota is named after people who dined and slept there and looked off across the lake towards my future boyhood home with—who knows, what thoughts?

Lewis Cass, the governor of Michigan Territory who inherited Minnesota after the war of 1812, and who eventually ran for President of the United States, passed through Sandy Lake in 1820 on an inspection tour of his new territory. Cass County is named after him. The Italian adventurer, Giacomo Beltrami, stayed here in 1823 on his way to the Red River. Beltrami County is named after him. Allen Morrison was actually the factor at the Sandy Lake post at the time of Beltrami's visit. Morrison County is named after him. William Aitkin managed the Sandy Lake post for a time after the American Fur Company took it over following defeat of the British in the war of 1812. Aitkin County is named after him. Joseph Nicollet passed through here in 1836 on his way to survey the Lake Itasca country. A county and a famous street in Minneapolis are named after him.

And of course it was a visitor from 150 years earlier, Sieur du Luth, whose name was appropriated by one of Minnesota's largest cities. Du

Luth's purpose in coming to Sandy Lake was partly to scout out the country, but primarily to make peace between the Sioux and Ojibwe so that fur trading could proceed without interference between warring tribes. It even appears as though this peace held for a time, until Lake Superior Ojibwes attacked Sioux villages on Sandy Lake and Lake Mille Lacs. From then on, there was only war.

Pike writes that the Sandy Lake post had been established 12 years prior to his visit in 1805, or in 1793. Apparently it was a large and important fort surrounded by a 100-foot-square stockade. When I was a boy of 12 or 13 no sign of the old fort remained, and once a week I unknowingly cut the grass atop its grave without knowing what ghosts I was disturbing in the process. One of the cabin owners on Browns Point whose grass I cut was a professor at Iowa State Teachers College named Irving Hart. Professor Hart spent his summers on Sandy Lake, apparently had time to spare, and eventually became an expert on the rich history of the Sandy Lake county. It was Hart, with the help of a Sandy Lake neighbor—a civil engineer named Ingersoll—who eventually retraced and marked the old Savannah Portage canoe route between Sandy Lake and Lake Superior.

Hart and Ingorsoll also calculated, based on the diaries of early fur traders, where the old fort had once stood on Browns Point. While the exact site of the vanished fort has come under question from later historians, Browns Point seems the likely location. In 1949, the year Minnesota celebrated its centennial as a Territory, the fort site was marked with a plaque and a centennial celebration was held on Browns Point. Professor Hart was the keynote speaker. I was there, hanging on every word, particularly when the good professor related how $50,000 in gold had gone to the bottom of Sandy Lake when a barge carrying this treasure had capsized. I was continually looking for the strongbox, and one time thought I had found it, but it turned out to be a rectangular-shaped box filled with cement which had once served as a boat anchor. So my excitement came to naught, though I continued searching, and I believe that every young boy should be so lucky as to grow up in the vicinity of lost treasure.

Following the war of 1812, the British no longer had fur trading rights in the United States and agreed to move their operations to Canada. Trouble was, nobody was quite certain where the border with Canada began, and the British continued to trade illegally at Sandy Lake until 1816, when the post was turned over to the American Fur Company under the head of John Jacob Astor. This American group operated the post for another six years, at which point the post was relocated to the confluence of the Sandy and Mississippi Rivers, quite near where the future town of Libby would eventually rise.

I have no idea why the post was moved to the river. Perhaps the old buildings were rotting away after 30 years of service. Perhaps a stockade was no longer needed. The fur trade had no doubt diminished, and quite possibly all major traffic was now north and south along the Mississippi rather than from Lake Superior. Perhaps there was very little trade to be had with the Sandy Lake Ojibwe following their cataclysmic encounters with smallpox and the Sioux.

At any rate, the old and famous fur trading post was moved to the vicinity of the Mississippi River, and I have reason to believe that its exact site is now beyond reach. Shortly before my father's death in 1999, he related how he had been taken to the site of the relocated fort by an old timer who then owned the property. Father recalled seeing stones and other debris consistent with a one-time building site. Unfortunately, this site, which lay directly north of the present Sandy River bridge, now lies buried beneath 30 feet of fill deposited there to raise highway 65 high above a flooding Mississippi. Does the old American Fur Company post now lie buried and forever beyond reach? No one will ever know for sure.

There is an interesting sequel to this Sandy Lake fur trading story. When French voyageurs dwelt or traveled in the proximity of an Ojibwe village there were bound to be children. History tells us that the French were popular with the Indians, possibly because they were inclined to adopt Indian customs and marry the daughters of Indian chieftains. In the early 1800's there were so many children of these mixed marriages at Sandy Lake that one Frederick Ayers started a mission school in 1832 to teach the children of his French voyaguers. He completed an Ojibwe spelling book—perhaps the first of its kind—and personally carried it to New York in 1833 to have it published. Another Sandy Lake visitor, Henry Schoolcraft, also published a book dealing with his travels among the Ojibwe. Both books may have been used by Longfellow in writing his famous epic poem, Hiawatha. Gitchi Gumi, after all, was the Ojibwe name for Lake Superior, and it was from those shores that our Sandy Lake Ojibwe came. No wonder I imagined the ghosts of Hiawatha and Minnehaha moving in birch bark canoes across the moonlit waters of my boyhood home.

Edmund Ely took up teaching duties at Sandy Lake in 1832 and remained four years before moving north to a now quite famous town that bears his name.

Also in 1832 another early schoolmaster named William Boutwell passed through Sandy Lake on his way to a teaching post on Leech Lake. Boutwell had been to Sandy Lake the year before with the Schoolcraft expedition, and now he was returning to Leech Lake from the Stillwater area with a new bride. The trip, according to Boutwell's journal, took 43 days of strenuous effort and must have been a most unusual honeymoon. Instead of ascending the Mississippi, the honeymooners traveled up the Brule River to Fond du Lac on Lake Superior (a 10 day journey), thence up the St Louis River to the Savannah River near present-day Floodwood, slogged through mud and mosquitoes across the seven-mile bog portage into the Prairie River, and thence into Sandy Lake.

I was puzzled why the honeymooners had taken this route to Sandy Lake rather than simply paddling up the Mississippi River, but apparently the approach from Lake Superior was considered the preferred route. The reasons are given in an 1820 letter from a Detroit official to

Louis Cass, then Governor of Michigan Territory, which included the Sandy Lake area. The official writes:

"There are two grand water communications with this country: one by Lake Superior and the Fond du Lac (St Louis) river, and the other by the Mississippi. The first is considered the most eligible route. It is about 1300 miles from St Louis to Sandy Lake, and 1050 miles from Detroit, by water, to the same place. There are many rapids on the Mississippi, particularly above the falls of St Anthony, which it is almost impossible to ascend by boats or canoes. The waters of this river are also unhealthy.

On the other course, the greatest difficulties are found in the rapids of the Fond du Lac River; but as this river is only ascended 150 miles, and the rapidity of the Mississippi continues for 600 miles, and a strong current the residue, the difference in the exertion and fatigue between the two routes is very great."

So there is the explanation. No wonder the Sioux at Elk River complained about the difficulty of ascending the Mississippi to attack the Ojibwe at Sandy Lake. I can well believe that the Sioux warriors were starved and exhausted by the time they arrived. The Lake Superior route was of course closed to the Sioux because of Ojibwe strongholds at Fond du Lac.

I was much impressed that the 1820 letter writer should know the distance—by water—from Sandy Lake to such important cities as Detroit and St Louis. It tells me that Sandy Lake was a very important place indeed—a place where great nations had once battled for dominance in the fur trade and for possession of North America.

My father, of course, knew nothing of this when he purchased his historic piece of lakeshore from Mr. Kay in 1934. The famous trading post had vanished. The Ojibwe village that had once stood on his very doorstep—the capital of a nation—lay swallowed by water backed up behind the Sandy Lake dam. Still, my father and his young bride must have felt the attraction of this ancient village site as they looked off across this island-studded lake, once a strategic gateway to interior Minnesota.

2

EARLIEST IMPRESSIONS

In November of 1935 my father drove his 17-year-old pregnant wife 65 miles to the nearest hospital in Brainerd where she was delivered of a 10 pound boy who is identified on the birth certificate only as "boy" Laursen. Perhaps my arrival in the world had happened too quickly, before they had mutually agreed on a permanent name. Or perhaps my mother and father disagreed on what the name should be until my sudden arrival forced a decision. At any rate, David I became, and I have been told many times by reliable sources that I quickly became the apple of my mother's eye. What was this new world of Sandy Lake like that I had so recently entered? Living in a store, with my father the postmaster, I must have gotten acquainted with our few neighbors very quickly as they arrived each day to pick up their mail. The store was in a rambling stucco building surrounded by our living quarters. To a child, the building seemed quite spacious. There were two bedrooms downstairs, two bedrooms upstairs, a kitchen, living and dining room, a glassed-in porch facing the lake, plus a laundry room in the rear. In the first years the house had no bathroom or running water and we all used the wooden two-hole outhouse on a hill behind the house. The house also had a small basement which held a wood-burning furnace and where canned goods were stored. The heat from the furnace rose by gravity through a two-foot by two foot metal floor register in the living room. It was amazing how many people could crowd onto this tiny space on cold winter mornings. The favorite room in the house on cold mornings was the kitchen where my mother cooked on an old-fashioned wood-burning cook stove. These were wonderful devices which not only cooked your food, but warmed the kitchen in the process, and heated water contained in a reservoir which lay adjacent to the firebox. It broke my stepmother's heart when father replaced it with a modern gas stove, though us children cheered because we were sick of carrying wood for the beastly thing. But no stove ever baked better pies, or had more useful surface area for canning vegetables, or was anywhere near as versatile overall.

The entrance to the store from our living quarters was through our kitchen. Upon entering the store, there was a small room to the right where father sorted mail and put it into the little combination lock boxes which could be accessed by their owner from the opposite side of the wall. To the left of the postal room was the store proper, a large open room which had shelves for canned goods along one wall, and a highly polished mahogany bar along another where beer and soft drinks were dispensed. Behind and under the bar were large metal coolers partially filled with water in which the beer and pop and bottles of milk were kept cool by blocks of ice floating in the water—similar in principle to our modern picnic coolers only on a grander scale. The coolers were perhaps six to eight-feet long and three feet wide, holding several cases of beer or soft drinks.

Behind the bar was a matching mahogany cabinet reaching from floor to ceiling and containing storage and display space for a host of items: cigarettes, round boxes of Copenhagen snoose, fishing tackle, lead sinkers, beef jerky, picture postcards, spools of fish line, patent medicines, and scores of items I can no longer remember. A few feet away stood two slot machines, or one-arm bandits, one of which accepted nickels, and the other dimes. These machines were popular with almost everyone until outlawed sometime in the 1940's. Rounding out the bar area were two or three wooden booths such as you see today in small town restaurants. Each would hold four people comfortably, and I spent many happy evenings with friends in such a contrivance drinking cokes and playing the same songs over and over on our jute box. Of course we had a juke box. In these days before television, it was the most important instrument in the store, and every few weeks the owner of the device would come around, remove the coins, and insert some new records. None too soon either, for our enjoyment of the old records was starting to pale. Whatever social life we had there on the lake in those years took place in those wooden booths, listening to our favorite songs on the juke box, to the triumphant clatter of nickels dropping to a winner at the slot machine, to the endless fishing and hunting stories swapped at the bar. The "regulars" at this bar were primarily our guests at the resort. Serious drinkers need not show up, because dad let them know in one way or another that they were not welcome. His philosophy was that it was unpleasant enough to stand behind a bar without having to listen to drunks. He was more tolerant of cabin guests who drank too much, but if they misbehaved beyond a certain point he never allowed them to return.

In the late 1930's we had electricity but it was used mainly for lighting, to operate the juke box and radio, and to power mother's wringer washing machine. There were no electric refrigerators, no electric motors, no power tools, electric dryers, water pumps, vacuum cleaners, or any other appliances now found in every home. Many of these devices existed, but we had no use for them. Our muscles were the power source and hand tools sufficed very well. If one should doubt this, consider that the immense virgin pine and hardwood forests of Minnesota were cut down and sawed into logs by hand in less than 40 years.

A single lane road followed the shore of the lake from a mile south and passed within perhaps 50 feet of our store, essentially through our front yard. This was no problem because cars in those days were few and hardly capable of more than a crawl. After all, this was practically the end of the road and there was really nowhere to go.

There was also an advantage in having the road pass through your front yard in that potential customers found it easier to stop than to drive on. And for anyone intending to continue north on the gravel trail that took one eventually to the iron range, ours was the last gas pump in 40 miles. By the time a traveler reached our store at the end of the tar road, their cars needed gas and probably oil, the car's radiator needed water which had either sloshed out or boiled away, the tires needed air if not patching, and the driver and passengers needed rest and refreshment. All of these amenities we could provide.

In later years my father built cabins between the road and the lake but during the time of which I speak the lakeshore was wooded with large oaks, unmowed, and pristine. And the mosquitoes were fierce. Directly across the road from the store was a path down a small hill to the water's edge where father had a half-dozen flat-bottomed boats which he rented to fisherman. Almost all fisherman rowed to their fishing spots and seldom had to row far to catch their limits of walleyes or northerns. In fact, it was easy to catch your limit right from our dock, and we usually had a cane pole there baited with a minnow with a cork to keep the bait off the bottom, and I remember catching fish all day long all summer long. A favorite fishing spot was the submerged river that flowed through our bay. The water there dropped off sharply from six feet to perhaps 15 feet and the fish followed the drop-off. Father had a raft of cedar logs positioned at the edge of the drop-off which attracted schools of large crappies averaging perhaps a pound and a half each. You could catch your limit early in the morning, or on nasty cloudy days they bit all day long. It was a favorite fishing spot of our guests, and even dad couldn't resist the lure of big crappies even though he seldom fished otherwise.

Beside and slightly behind the store were the four cabins my father had purchased from Mr. McKay as part of the resort. The cabins were unique in that none of them bore any resemblance to the others, and were constructed of different materials and perhaps at different times. DeerLodge, so named because it had a set of deer antlers over the door, was built of vertical logs, with the gaps between the logs stuffed with oakum and morter. The other cabins—Tumble Inn, Bide-a-wee, and Just Married—were built of unplaned local lumber. Their only common element was a screened-in porch facing the lake in which hung a wooden swing that held two adults or three or four children. A screened-in porch was more essential in those days to a guest's happiness than an indoor toilet or running water, mainly because of the hordes of mosquitoes which made life outside in the evenings quite impossible. The swings in the porches were also popular, and in the evening silence one could hear the rhythmic squeak of the chains on which the swings hung as the guests swung back and forth, back and forth, in the deepening twilight.

We had a number of close neighbors to the south, but to the north there was only one—the Corp of Engineers employee who tended the locks and gates on the Sandy Lake dam. We called him simply the damtender, and he lived in a government-owned house beside the spillway on some beautiful grounds which gave him a sweeping view of the lake as well as the Sandy River.

At one time the locks had been used to allow steamboats to pass between the lake and the river, but steamboat traffic had ceased before I was born, and I never saw the locks being used for that purpose. The dam also contained three or four manually operated gates which could be opened to let excess water out of the lake. There was also a cement fish ladder which allowed spawning fish to climb a series of watery steps from the river into the lake, which was a wonderful sight to see in the Spring as thousands of fish of all species congregated below the dam in numbers so dense that you had the impression you could cross the river walking on their backs. This annual fish migration restocked the lake every year, and the fishing both above and below the dam was a spectacle to behold. In later years the fishladder was removed out of fears that carp migrating up the Mississippi would get into the lake and destroy the wild rice beds. This strategy succeeded in keeping out the carp, but it kept out the migrating gamefish also, and fishing went downhill in a hurry.

The dam destroyed the fishery in other ways also—through mismanagement of water levels which led to repeated years of flooding in the 1950's. This flooding, after eventually receding, left Sandy Lake's spawning fish high and dry in the swamps of McGregor and Tamarack. Between the closing of the fishladder on the Sandy Lake dam and the loss of breeding stock through disastrous floods, the fishing on Sandy Lake was never as good afterwards.

This repeated flooding led to an ongoing battle between my father and the Corp of Engineers which took years to resolve. The problem was due to differing views as to the purpose of a dam, and also to changes in the world since the dam was built. The dam, after all, had not been built to improve the beauty of Sandy Lake, but to create a reservoir of water which could be released downstream in periods of drought to keep the Mississippi River deep enough to float steamboats and power the turbines which ground the wheat and powered the sawmills in the Twin Cities.

When steamboat traffic ceased on the Upper Mississippi and the sawmills went silent with the demise of the white pine forests, the dams built on Sandy Lake, Pokegama, Leech, and Winne were still there. Some new use had to be found for the impounded water to justify the existence of the dams as well as the dam's owners—the Army Corp of Engineers.

And a new use for the water was soon found—to slake the thirst of Twin Cities residents. If Mississippi River water was no longer needed to float steamboats or power sawmills, at least the citizens downstream might drink it. The water could also be caught and held by other dams on the river itself which could be released as needed to facilitate barge traffic between St Paul and St Louis.

With this in mind, the main purpose of Sandy Lake and the other northern reservoirs became simply to hold back water—which meant keeping the reservoirs as full as possible. But this philosophy led to immediate problems. A reservoir—once full—can not hold more water without the water going somewhere. In particular, a full reservoir cannot hold the spring runoff, or accommodate abnormally heavy summer rains. This is particularly true of a lake like Big Sandy which drains a large part of Aitkin County. In its pre-dam era, Sandy Lake was surrounded by vast bogs and wild rice beds which could temporarily absorb unusually heavy rains or snow melt. Now there was nowhere for the water to go. The Sandy Lake dam could not release the water fast enough to control the lake level, nor was it possible to release water into an already flooded Mississippi. Compounding the problem was the fact that Sandy Lake had become a popular recreation area. People were building cabins and resorts close to the water on a lake that was already full to the brim. Much of the building had taken place over a period of dry years. Newcomers had no idea what would happen to their level and lovely lakeshore lots once the rains returned. Big Sandy Lake was a disaster waiting to happen.

In March of 1950 a Spring blizzard swept east off Lake Superior to bury our home and the one-lane road along the lake under drifts four to five feet deep. Conventional snowplows could not break through. We were snowed in and cut off from the outside world. Travel anywhere was possible only on snowshoes. The snow was so deep that father did not attempt to shovel it. There was no work for me and no school—nothing to do but walk atop the deep snow on snowshoes, which produced an exhilaration similar to the ability to walk on water. A school friend who lived miles to the north came down on snowshoes to meet me, and we had a wonderful time. The world we had known was buried, and there was a strange and exciting new world to explore.

In a few weeks the deep snow melted and filled the many streams draining into Sandy Lake. Practically the whole of Aitkin Country was under water, one large lake as it had been in the days of Glacier Lake Aitkin. Sandy Lake and its surrounding bogs were full of water, and more was flowing in every day. It crept into the front yards of the cabin owners and finally into the cabins themselves. Those cabins that were not fastened down floated away. The water flooded into the cattail bogs, lifting the bogs and wrenching off great chunks which floated off across the lake willy nilly. The well traveled channel between Aitkin Lake and Big Sandy disappeared completely one day, blocked by a floating bog, to the utter confusion of fisherman trying to return to their cabins on Sandy Lake.

The high waters receded finally, doing a tremendous amount of damage to property, spawning beds, and destroying the wild rice crop for a number of years in succession, which affected waterfowl nesting and their fall migration. Everyone was willing to write off the floods of 1950 as an aberration, except that it happened again the next year, and the next, and the next. It was obvious that something was wrong, and father blamed the dam. If the lake level were drawn down in the fall, he argued, then the lake would be capable of holding the spring runoff. Not so, said the Corp of Engineers. They were not to blame for the flooding. It was mother nature's fault, plus the oxbow bends in the Mississippi River which did not let the water escape south fast enough. A flood diversion project was started in the Aitkin area to straighten out some of these bends and this no doubt helped.

But the real problem was one of philosophy—how full to keep the reservoirs. The Corp of Engineers had the same attitude towards water as the beaver—the more water the better. Water was their money in the bank, so to speak. The more they had, the longer they could spend it. This meant keeping all the northern reservoirs as full as possible. Father disagreed, and insisted they draw down the reservoirs in the fall and winter. Father had the support of local property owners and in the mid-1950's they banded together and formed the Big Sandy Lake Improvement Association, with my father as its first president. Thus began a battle with the Corp of Engineers that went all the way to the United States Senate and took the intervention of Hubert Humphrey and others to get the Corp of Engineers to change their ways. There have been no floods of consequence since.

The dam tenders at the Sandy Lake dam were our friends and good enough fellows. We did not hold them responsible for orders emanating out of Corp Headquarters in St Paul and St Louis. Mr. McKay, who had built my father's resort, had been himself one of the early damtenders, and had been in charge of the locks in 1924 when a flotilla of steam launches had voyaged upriver and passed through the dam into Sandy Lake. Mr. McKay was apparently a visionary who saw a brighter future in the tourist business than as a government bureaucrat. He was also visionary enough to sell out, perhaps realizing that the tourist business was still many years off. The trouble with most visionaries is that their timing is off. Much of Sandy Lake was owned over the years by various speculators who were right about the boom, but disastrously wrong in its timing.

The earliest dam tender I remember as a child was a tall, gaunt fellow by the name of Henry Dart. Each morning Mr. Dart would march down the road in front of our store with long and purposeful strides, arms swinging, his back ramrod straight, looking neither to the right or the left, his visit to the water gauges as predictable as a fox to its favorite scent trees. There were two water gauges that I recall, one just down the road from our house on the lakeshore and another on the Mississippi River which required a half-mile hike through the woods. The water gauges of which I speak looked like large metal culverts sunk vertically into the water close to shore with rocks piled around their base to keep the culvert standing upright. The culvert had a locked door and a ladder inside down which the damtender could climb and read the level of the lake off a calibrated rod that projected up from the lake bottom. Any rise or fall of the lake was reflected by the water level in the culvert, and could be compared from one day to another by means of the calibrated gauge. Having the gauge inside the culvert protected it from vandalism and the effects of wave action. I am no longer sure how often these water readings were taken, but I would not be surprised if—in some obscure vault or warehouse somewhere—there are not thousands of pages of recordings of Sandy Lake water levels, rainfall, and temperature data going back nearly a century.

The most interesting water gauge to me was the one on the Mississippi River a half-mile behind our house just south of the old steamboat landing where the Sandy joined the Mississippi River. For some reason, the gauge had been put on the west bank of the river, which prevented one from reaching it on foot. In the days of the steamboats the river was the highway so it did not really matter which side of the river held the water gauge. Now it did, because there were no roads close to the river on its west bank.

One could reach the water gauge by boat in summer, but during much of the winter the river was partially iced over, and even when frozen completely across would seldom support a man's weight, as Zebulon Pike discovered on his search for the source of the Mississippi more than a century before.

The Corp of Engineers at some point solved this dilemma by stringing a cable across the river and mounting upon it a tiny wooden cable car, painted white, upon which two people could sit facing each other. The cable car was manually operated in some fashion but I never understood just how the damtender managed to pull himself across the river. Since the cable sagged in the center, the car would roll to the center of the river under the force of gravity, but then the damtender would require some means of pulling himself the rest of the way. Since I never caught him stranded in the center of the river, such means evidently existed.

I never did penetrate the mystery of the cable car, but not because I failed to try. Many times I climbed into the seat and pretended that I was pulling myself hand over hand across the river, or stranded somewhere in the middle dangling over some bottomless abyss, the strands of cable parting one by one until only a single strand remained to prevent my plunge into the alligator infested river far below. Fortunately for me, the cable car was always locked up tight, and I was never there at the right time to cajole Mr. Dart into taking me for a ride.

At other times I stood beside the cable car and looked upriver a few hundred yards to the vanished town of Libby which had once stood on the tree-covered peninsula between the two rivers. The forest had reclaimed the village site totally, and only a heap of rocks on the riverbank remained of the once busy piers. In 1906 five different steamboats were plying this stretch of the river between Brainerd and Grand

Rapids. In that year alone 5500 passengers passed this spot, and 12,000 tons of freight. Now there was only silence.

In the middle of the last century a lone and terrified Ojibwe boy had leaped from his canoe very near this place and ran for his life, pursued by a flotilla of Sioux war canoes. The Sioux warriors had come up river from Elk River to attack the Ojibwe village on Sandy Lake. Their surprise attack would have succeeded, but they stopped to chase some Ojibway girls picking blueberries along the river. The fleeing Ojibwe boy had been with the blueberry pickers, or close by, and was now running for his life to warn the Sandy Lake village before the Sioux warriors arrived. The boy arrived ahead of the Sioux, but the men in the village had just returned from a celebration with relatives at Fond du Lac and were all sleeping off a drunk. The women somehow were able to shake the groggy men awake, and stick guns in their hands. The surprise attack was foiled by the boy, and the village saved.

Between the steamboat days and the Indian wars the lumbermen arrived with their two-man cross-cut saws and began cutting the pine forests beside the river and all its tributaries. If I had been standing at this site in the 1890's in the Spring of the year I could have watched two massive log drives—one coming down the Mississippi River from the north, and the other coming from Sandy Lake on the east. Then the river would have rang with shouts as the river men worked the logs around the shoals and rapids with their peeveees and off the slippery, muddy banks. A river of logs it was in the spring, and following the logs, or in their midst, was the floating wanigan, or cookshack, where the rivermen took their meals. The white pine floated high in the water, but the red or Norway pine tended to get waterlogged and sink, which probably explains where the word "waterlogged" came from. Nearly fifty years after the log drives the river was still so full of half sunken pine logs that my father snaked them home behind a boat and outboard motor, hired a sawmill, and had the logs sawed into good pine lumber from which he built a fine barn. There remain sunken logs in the river to this day, as sound as the day they were cut because wood does not decay under water. The water, however, changes the chemical composition of the wood in some way, creating some strikingly beautiful patterns. I read once that Stradivari fashioned his wonderful violins from logs taken from the water, the waterlogged wood with its changed chemical composition responsible for the distinctive tone of his violins.

Standing beside the locked-up cable car looking north towards the vanished town of Libby, the river is silent and had been silent for nearly fifty years. Gone are the Indian canoes, the furtraders, the explorers and missionaries, the lumbermen, the farmers and homesteaders with their wives and children—wave after wave of widely different people fighting their way upstream against the current of this watery highway. All heading north for different reasons. All gone now.

When I was a boy only a few fisherman occasionally visited this spot where the Sandy River emptied into the Mississippi. And then only in early spring or fall when the mosquitoes were absent. This was a wonderful fishing hole, here where the Sandy joined the Mississippi. On the east side of the river, just across from the old town, was a grassy bank which once was the front yard of an old homestead. The homestead itself had collapsed into a pile of weathered logs mixed with the droppings of porcupines. But the grassy bank between the ruined house and the river was a wonderful place to sit and fish. I sat there often with my Uncle Tom, a long cane pole in my lap, the spinner on the end of my line baited with a lively shiner minnow. Just across the river was an old rock pier where steamboats had once tied up, only the boulders still remaining of which many had rolled into deeper water, creating perfect structure to attract walleyes and rock bass.

We caught many walleyes off that grassy bank on lazy summer afternoons, almost all of them on the long cane poles which remain one of the most effective fishing instruments ever created. Gone now is the grassy bank, and the log ruins of the unknown homesteader, and the boys with canepoles. These "barefoot boys with cheeks of tan" with their canepoles immortalized by Longfellow have vanished just as surely as the Indian, the furtrader, the logger, and all the rest who had their brief season on this particular stretch of river.

◆   ◆   ◆

Whereas the damtender was our only neighbor to the north, we had several neighbors to the south who lived in year-around homes facing the lake. These people—all of whom were retired—could rightfully be called residents of the town of Libby. These people must have come into the country with a certain amount of money, for they built large, square, two-story homes with fieldstone fireplaces—all of which are still standing and remain fine homes today. There were three of these large homes directly south of us, all built on a hill that grew steeper as one went south. These oldtimers knew enough to build on high ground, perhaps even then familiar with the capricious water levels of Sandy Lake following construction of the dam. The inhabitants of these three homes—our closest neighbors—changed from time to time as I was growing up, but they were all fine people who had a profound influence on my life.

The third house to the south was occupied by a retired school superintendent by the name of T.B. Morris. The Morris house sat on a thirty-foot bluff with the road passing directly below. Across the road, down another 15-foot bank, was the lake itself and the submerged point of land where the Ojibwe village had once stood. Now, the village site was simply a sandbar stretching far out into the bay where we went swimming on warm summer days.

I was in and out of the Morris house many times, for Mrs. Morris had befriended my young mother and I suspect my mother visited the home often with me in tow. Little did I know then how important this house on the cliff would become as I grew older.

Mr. and Mrs. Morris were already very old when I made their acquaintance. Mr. Morris was in his eighties, a taciturn and frightening creature to me, tall and gaunt as Ichabod Crane. If he ever spoke to me

I don't recall it. He taught me nothing, offered no advice that I am aware of, yet this old schoolmaster had a major influence on my education. For when Mr. Morris moved to the end of the road to retire he brought along a wonderful library of books which now lined the walls of the living room in his big house. I don't know how old I was when I discovered the books, and gained access to them, but that day changed my life and opened up an unsuspected world of beauty, excitement, and adventure. This discovery must have happened quite young because my mother taught me to read before I started school. By the time I was nine or ten I was able to read anything I could get my hands on.

The guardian of this treasure trove of books was the schoolmaster's wife, Mrs. T.B. Morris. Mrs. Morris was already an invalid by the time I knew her, confined to a rocking chair where she reportedly stayed day and night. She had a variety of ailments—dropsy being the one I recall—though today we would probably call it congestive heart failure.

Despite being an invalid, Mrs. Morris was always very patient and kind to me. She had loved my dead mother, and no doubt felt sorry for my sister and I. She doled out the books as I requested them, and no doubt understood the kind of books I would like, for the books she gave me were exciting fare indeed—far more interesting than the books available in the library at school. My favorites were the Tarzan books written by Edgar Rice Burroughs. I reread them again and again and they are still wonderful reading today, besides being collectors items. Most of the books I collect today are books that filled the shelves of the Morris house. I have often marveled at my good fortune to have been set down in the woods near the end of the road next to a library of books. It reminds me of the weasel who makes her home in the carcass of a deer—all the necessary substance close at hand. My mother died at 23 leaving me essentially alone but not without resources. The books became my mother, father, sister, brother. As my dead mother looked down from eternity I believe she must have gotten great satisfaction to see me travel so joyfully and far in the world of books. The poet Keats called this "traveling in the realms of gold" and so it was.

My mother would have understood my joy in books because she was a reader too. Part of her trousseau when she moved to Sandy Lake as a young bride of 17 was a box or two of books. I know they were her own personal books because her name was written inside the cover. After her death the boxes found their way into the attic and I discovered them there by spying on my father. One day, when he decided I was old enough to read it, he handed me a book called "The Branding Iron." For some reason I assumed the book had come from the Morris house, and tried to return it there, but they disclaimed all knowledge of it. I gave the book back to my father and must have watched where he put it, or perhaps he told me, but I soon discovered the hiding place. Off my father's bedroom in our rambling old house was a trapdoor in the wall which led to an attic. Once you entered the attic, there was a hole in the ceiling through which you could lower yourself unto another level of the attic. The boxes of books were there, under the eaves, a cozy place indeed. I visited that attic often with my flashlight in secret because it was not a place I was supposed to be. A single misstep could send me crashing through the ceiling into the store below.

I found I could read quite well by flashlight, and would read under the covers after I had been sent to bed. Grandmother Clemmer heard about this in some way and—fearful that I would ruin my eyes—sent me a fine lantern for reading under the covers. Once my father learned the lantern's true purpose, he took the lantern away, and reading under the covers became a forbidden activity.

Still, I managed to find plenty of time to read. Many of the books I enjoyed most were simply an extension of the life I was already living. I was an offspring of the northern forest, but the books of London and Curwood took place even further north—in that mysterious horizon I could see for myself whenever I looked north. But unlike my own life—which I saw as unrelenting labor and loneliness—these books were filled with love, danger, riches beyond imagination, and freedom.

They were peopled with strong characters who had all the virtues I admired: strength, courage, honor, integrity, vast endurance, unconditional love. The good guys and the bad guys were clearly defined, and the bad guys always lost in the end.

Life would have been bleak indeed without the books. They added spice and possibility to a life that for the most part was unrelieved labor. We heated our rambling house and store with a wood furnace which had a voracious appetite. On every winter weekend Sis and I would spend a full day filling our basement with wood from floor to ceiling, and this mountain of wood would have disappeared into the furnace by the next weekend. The kitchen cookstove also burned wood, and though it devoured smaller pieces, this took even more work in that the cookstove wood needed to be split into kindling, and be thoroughly sound and dry before it would pass muster with the cook. The kitchen woodbox was small and required filling every day. Woe to us if the woodbox was empty when the cook went to start her morning fire.

If it was not firewood demanding our attention it was the water bucket. All water—for drinking as well as washing—came from a handpump in the yard which gave up its treasure most reluctantly. Each pull on the pumphandle yielded hardly more than a cupfull, some of which would go in the pail when a strong northwest wind was blowing. The remainder of the cupful would freeze on your pantsleg, not only making your leg stiff with cold, but encasing it in a sheath of ice which prevented you from bending your leg at the knee. On wash-days, when it was necessary to fill the washing machine and two large tubs with water, one might spend an hour or two pumping frantically or in slow despair, depending on your mood at the time. No wonder we learned to dread Sunday afternoons, when Monday's washwater needed to be pumped. Eventually, of course, we got an electric pump and a deeper well which father and I dug mostly by hand.

No wonder we preferred school to staying at home. Attending school was a joy and a blessing—a momentary surcease from painful labor. School holidays were a thing to be dreaded—particularly the Christmas holiday when we would cut and pack away the hundreds of blocks of ice needed to keep our iceboxes cool during the coming summer. This would be preceded by several days of shoveling snow—shoveling roads to the icehouse, roads out onto the lake, roads everywhere it seemed. There were no snowblowers in those days and we did not own a tractor with a snowplow. So dad and I would shovel wherever we needed to go. We might spend three solid days shoveling snow to get up to our icehouse. To a boy this seemed like labor without end, equivalent to the classic tale of forever rolling a boulder to the top of a mountain. With such a task before us I remember feeling only a kind of hopeless resignation. The job was impossible. It would take forever. I would spend the rest of my life shoveling snow. Strangely enough, once the mind accepted the hopelessness of the situation, it somehow became bearable. You simply bowed your head and kept at it without doing very much thinking about it. Perhaps this was the secret of the plantation slave, or prisoners in the Gulag—a survival technique to get you through the day.

But eventually the job always got done, hope returned, and I learned a wonderful lesson from these ordeals which proved useful many times in later life. When faced with a seemingly impossible task, don't stop working and don't think. Just keep at until the job is done. Our rational mind is the body's best friend, or its worst enemy, as the case may be. Every battle is won or lost in the mind first.

Looking back, I believe my upbringing would have won the approval of Plato himself. The Greeks saw the total human being as a combination of body, mind, and spirit—all of which required the proper cultivation. Each of these parts of me were cultivated, whether I liked it or not.

There was unrelenting physical work to create physical and mental toughness. There were books to feed the soul and fire the imagination. There was loss and grief which produced a certain stoicism and fatalistic view of life.

Undoubtedly the most traumatic event in my life was the loss of my mother to cancer at age 23 when I was five years old. She was a young, warm, and loving person. My sister Ann and I were the joys of her life. We grew up basking in the warmth of her love and then suddenly she was snatched away, leaving us with a harsh and grief-stricken father in a harsh and lonely environment.

I dreamed my mother's death long before it happened—a recurring dream from which I would wake crying and terrified. It seems to me that these dreams started before she became ill, but I am not sure about that. Perhaps this was prescience, or intuition, or perhaps I heard things whispered in the dead of the night. She was far away at the Mayo clinic when she finally died and Ann and I were not told of her death until some weeks or months afterwards.

When her end was near (we were not told this, of course), Father took Ann and I to visit her at the Mayo. Though only five years of age at the time, I can remember that visit clearly, perhaps because it was the first time I saw my father weep, and was surprised that he could. My mother was lying in bed, and Ann and I went to her to be hugged. We had already been separated for some time, and perhaps there was already some reserve in us, some unknown fear, as she stretched out her arms and bid us come. I believe father, through his tears, had to order us to go forward.

For a long time afterwards her absence seemed only like a bad dream, but eventually we accepted the truth that she was not coming home.

What does a young and loving mother say to her young children on her deathbed? Not very much, I fear. The pain is too great for words, and words cannot embrace the horror of it. Given a choice, most mothers would rather die than abandon their young children. But now there was to be no choice. It was to be both death and abandonment. Did God reassure and comfort her in this moment of overwhelming grief, as He has comforted me from time to time over the course of my life? I suspect He did. The Lord can speak very clearly to us when He chooses, and the effect is miraculous. To me at least, the words were these: "It's going to be alright." More than once I heard those words, and the words were true. I believe He must have said those words to my dying mother, but He was not saying them to me at that time.

But Ann and I were not left totally comfortless. Within two years father married Irene Enderle, a fine woman who had taken care of Ann and I in my mother's absence. We knew and loved her but she was not yet our mother and the great void in our lives remained for a long time. A mother's love and nurturing is apparently not just physical. Some spiritual connection had been severed, and this connection was irreplaceable. Like a missing limb, the source of the pain was gone, but the pain remained.

Some of this spiritual connection remained and was provided by my mother's two sisters and her own mother, who at this time was around sixty years of age. These sisters and mother had loved my mother—she was the baby of the family—and they were brokenhearted by her death. Ann and I were the children of their baby sister, and they did their best to help us know and remember our mother—her pride in us, her dreams for our future. This second-hand vision may have been scanty fare, but it was what my sister and I desperately needed—the unconditional love that only a family member can provide, a time of dwelling in the center of somebody's universe. My aunts and my grandmother provided that kind of unconditional love and for that I will be forever grateful.

The two years or so following my mother's illness and death I can only dimly remember. There was a procession of hired men and women who watched over us when my father was away at the hospital, or working. These people were no doubt kind, but they were strangers, and neither Ann or I particularly liked them.

My mother's sister, Donna, and my Uncle Tom—two of my favorite people—were taking care of us at our Sandy Lake home when the Armistice Day blizzard struck on my birthday on November 7, 1941. Father was apparently away at the hospital. Tom recalls that no wood had been gathered that fall—perhaps because of mother's illness—and he remembers struggling to find wood under three feet of snow to heat the house. That fall had been unusually warm. The blizzard had struck unexpectedly, killing many late-season duck hunters who had gone hunting that day inadequately dressed for the bone-chilling cold and snow about to pounce from the northwest. Perhaps uncle Tom had been busy with other projects, and had put off the gathering of wood until it was too late.

This truly must have been a time to try my father's soul. He had lost his young wife and helpmate, leaving him alone in a new land with two young children. A month after that tragic blizzard the Japanese attacked Pearl Harbor, propelling the United States into the second Great War. The world was still in the depths of the Great Depression. Between death, war, and economic collapse, the Four Horseman of the Apocalypse were all riding except perhaps for Pestilence. I do not know the tenor of my father's thoughts during that dark period, but I am grateful that he was one of those men of indomitable will who refuse to remain defeated for long.

Certainly he must have seen his life as a defeat at that time. And there is no question that this experience left him scarred and somewhat bitter. He was now a widower, probably penniless, with a roof over his head but few prospects. He must have worried a great deal over how he was to take care of his two young children. Did he have fears that well meaning people might attempt to take his children away? He never admitted to this, but such concerns must have crossed his mind? At any rate, he kept my sister and I very close at hand, only rarely allowing us to visit our dead mother's relatives. Perhaps he feared that they would attempt to keep us, or turn us against him. To their great credit, they never did.

I say this is to their credit because my mother's relatives had no cause to love my father. He had taken their baby sister when hardly more than a child and hauled her far off to a primitive place, where she takes sick and dies while still a young girl. Did my mother's family blame my father to a certain extent for my mother dying young? Did my father believe that they blamed him? Did he blame himself? But perhaps there was no blame on either side. Her death was a tragedy pure and simple and life must go on. Upon reading my mother's letters to her own mom, it is very clear that she loved and was proud of my father and excited about their future. "Olaf will be rich some day," she wrote in her letters.

If there were people who believed that father was not suited to raising two young children, they must have held their peace. And it is easy to understand why. Father was a very intimidating person. He had not only great physical strength but a frightening temper and was absolutely fearless. When in one of his rages nobody knew for sure to what lengths he would go—murder not excepted—and he kept them guessing, deliberately, I suspect, perhaps smiling to himself all the while. I say he was deliberate about this because he was not reckless. He knew when to hold his tongue and whose favor he needed. He knew the bankers and the local politicians, paid his bills promptly, and had the support and respect of the local business community. I'm not sure just how he made these friends in the right places because he did not attempt to curry favor. His secret, I believe, is that he was always straight and direct with people so they knew exactly where he stood. The people he despised knew they were despised, and hated him for it. Conversely, those he respected knew they were respected, and admired his powers of discrimination.

During this dark period following my mother's death my father made a momentous decision—to stay put at his Sandy Lake home. This too could not have been an easy decision. The war had started, and good jobs were becoming available. Why not leave this place of tears and bitter memories forever? Why not give up his young children to caring relatives and start anew? He was in the prime of life and could easily have done so without being blamed.

Did he stay because of some promise made to my mother on her deathbed? Did she make him promise not to leave her young children in the care of strangers? Did she tell him to stay put and be a man? To continue to pursue their shared dream of a home on Sandy Lake? Perhaps he promised my dying mother all these things and more.

But perhaps his decision to stay put was based on more mundane reasons. He told me once that he had sat down with pencil and paper and calculated that all he needed to make was a dollar a day to be better off at Sandy Lake than at a higher paying job in a distant city. Here his overhead was low: no fuel bills, low taxes, no house payment—but he was $50,000 in debt due to my mother's medical bills—a staggering sum for those days. It took years, but eventually those bills were paid in full.

But how was he to make that dollar a day he needed? The devil here was certainly in the details, and he ended up trying a little bit of everything. He had a small income as postmaster, and some uncertain income from the resort and store. But this was not enough to support a family, and also get ahead. His American Dream did not include standing still.

So he built a large barn, acquired a herd of milk cows, and became a dairy farmer as well as a resort owner. He purchased a flatbed truck in 1936 and began cutting virgin oaks on his 40 acres near Aitkin Lake which eventually were sawed into railroad ties. The oaks were so large that some logs produced four ties per log. He rented some bottomlands along the Mississippi River to the north and tried raising flax for three or four years until floods and insects forced him to give it up. Then he raised potatoes in large fields which he plowed and cultivated with a team of horses. The result of this Herculean effort was plenty of potatoes to eat but not much money.

Despite the failed crops and backbreaking work, father must have made his dollar-a-day objective. The dairy herd was growing, and with it a larger milk check from the creamery at Palisade. More tourists were coming north to fish despite their pre-war cars and gas rationing.

During these war years we not only managed to survive, but father was able to make an improvement here and there—a new boat, a new cabin, a new well—all built with his own hands (and mine, such as they were).

If we needed a septic system, we dug it by hand. The same with a new well. Lumber to build our cabins was sawed from logs we had cut ourselves on the Aitkin Lake property, or pulled from the river. We heated with wood and cooled ourselves and our customers in summer with blocks of ice we had personally cut from the lake during the winter. Our labor for the most part substituted for cash, though some cash money was needed.

It is difficult to imagine how much time was spent in simply trying to stabilize the temperature of the surrounding environment—keeping warm, keeping your food cool, feeding the physical machine which is our body with enough fuel to perform at the high energy level required. Fat people among laborers in the country were a rarity indeed. These labors of which I speak were unrelenting, backbreaking, but surprisingly—totally satisfying. No joy can compare with the joy of a peaceful rest following Herculean labor, a hearty meal and a full stomach earned by the sweat of your brow. This joy is available now mainly through our recreation—biking, canoeing, backpacking—but once it was available to almost everyone through their work. Some writer called those of my age the "last fit generation,"—people who stayed lean through hard work before sedentary lifestyles turned even our young towards obesity. Nobody, I suspect, would desire to return to those days of unrelenting physical labor. We were no better than workhorses engaged in repetitive slave labor. But oh, how wonderful it was when the pain ceased for a day.

This backbreaking labor eventually took its toll on my father. He slipped a disc or two in his back hand-lifting 400 pound oak logs and was incapacitated, literally unable to get out of bed. South to the Mayo Clinic he went once again. In an experimental kind of surgery, the doctors carved a slice of bone from my father's leg and fused it to the spine in some way, stabilizing the slipping vertebrae. The surgery was successful and alleviated the back pain. However, the doctors told him to find another occupation. No more lifting for him. His days of physical labor were over. Or so the doctors ordered. But father had his own ideas. He bought a stiff corset to stabilize his back and went back to heavy lifting for the next forty years as though nothing had happened. At age 90 I suspect he could still outlift his doctors, assuming that any were still alive.

But the bad back undoubtedly cooled his ardor for continuing as a logger. And low blood iron bordering on anemia perhaps got us out of the dairy business. When our dairy herd had grown to perhaps 15 milk cows, father got an infection in a minor scratch and blood poisoning set in. Back to the Mayo Clinic he went and they just managed to save his arm and his life. My stepmother, myself, and a hired man carried on the milking in my father's absence, but once he recovered the herd was sold. Perhaps his bout with illness showed him that he was spread too thin—that to succeed at anything he needed to focus on something. The logging, the potato farming, the flax growing, the dairy farming—all had been tried and found wanting, but had served a temporary purpose. Now, with the war ended, and gasoline once again available for ordinary travel, tourists were beginning to come north again in larger numbers, and in a host of new and exciting looking automobiles—the first built since before the war. The time had finally come to focus on the resort business.

3

THE SUMMER PEOPLE

In 1945 the war in Europe ended with the Russians storming Berlin, and Hitler's suicide in a Berlin bunker with the Russians only a block or two away. Later that summer the Japanese surrendered after atomic bombs practically obliterated Hiroshima and Nagasaki. Much soul searching takes place today as to whether the bombs should have been dropped, but there were few such doubts at the time. The Japanese were a brutal, fanatic, and implacable foe. They had killed thousands of young American men and would kill thousands more if the islands of Japan had to be invaded in the conventional way. The atomic bomb undoubtedly saved many lives—both American and Japanese—and Japan was far less devastated than German cities had been though conventional bombing and street-to-street fighting.

The period when the war ended was a time of tremendous positive energy, pride, and hope for the future. We had defeated a powerful and evil enemy, confirmed our belief that good ultimately wins out over evil, and that God—in this conflict, at least—was on our side. We were the world champs, so to speak—winners of the ultimate Super-Bowl—with all the joy, madness, and exhilaration that such winners enjoy.

After five years of yielding up our freedom to fight for our common survival, the battle was over, and we were once again free—as frisky as confined calves turned out of the barn for the first time in the Spring. All the rationing—of gasoline and everything else—was over. People could travel where they liked, eat what they liked, and most important—had the money to do it. The soldiers came home, got married, and had the children immortalized on Ozzie and Harriet.

This was the world I awoke to after the long dark winter of war, depression, and my mother's death. I was seeing the world for the first time, or with new eyes, or it was in fact a new world. I suppose it was all these things.

What changed my life most profoundly was the arrival at our resort of the summer people—our guests, who also became our closest friends. During the war we had a few fishermen coming to the resort, but now the fishermen came with their wives, and with their children. The impact of these people on my lonely life was like rain to the desert. They came with their strange faces and their new and strange ideas, telling tales of faraway places. But what brought the greatest joy to my life was their children. I had playmates at school, of course, but none close by—and now, for the first time in my life, I had friends to spend the summers with.

These summer friendships were not ideal, of course, for they only lasted a week, or two at the most—but what wonderful weeks they were! A week in a child's life is an age—quite long enough to establish deep and genuine friendships. It took perhaps a day to make friends with a stranger, and for the next week you rode the heights of happiness, and then your new friend left, plunging you into the profoundest gloom. The separation was like death in the family all over again. I remember walking around the resort after certain friends left in a state of profound grief, the world once again an empty and lonely place. It was a constant emotional roller coaster, and the pain of those separations probably made it difficult for me to seek out friendships throughout my life. If one has to choose between loneliness and separation, loneliness is the lesser pain.

I was too young at the time to be interested in girls because they were girls. Girls had an added mystery about them, but my relationships with them were almost identical to those with my male friends. These children, whether male or female, were my friends, confidents, and soulmates. We were as bold and adventuresome as any Huck Finns or Tom Sawyers. Because it was usually just them and me, there were no competing playmates vying for attention, no petty jealousies, no time for falling out and making up. These children were strangers in a new and strange world, and I was the guide. They had come to the lake, perhaps in protest, prepared to be bored, and were amazed to find companions in the depths of the forest who were intelligent, interesting, and knew of many things which our city visitors did not. Ours was a different set of attitudes, hobbies, wild animals, and basic fears. Rowing a boat, cleaning a fish, milking a cow, raking up mounds of rotting mayflies off the beach—these were all new and strange activities to most. Hide and Seek took on new meaning where the hiding places were infinite, and perhaps even dangerous. What monsters existed in the shadow of oaks and hazelbrush, in the depths of the cattail bog? What treasures could compare with the discovery of wild strawberries, raspberries, blackberries, hazelnuts?

A week or two with a new friend in such circumstances forever changed their life and yours. Your hearts were sad and heavy when they went home, or at least mine was. They were returning to their home and old friends, but I was staying behind, all the happy places which so recently had rang with our excited talk, empty now and silent. My loneliness was profound. The cabin people turned over once a week and perhaps a new friend would arrive. Quite often they did, and the cycle of getting acquainted, joyful play, and painful separation would repeat itself.

Some of these playmates returned the following year, and some for several years thereafter. But the relationships were seldom the same. A year's growth in size or experience had changed something irrevocably. There were new constraints and expectations in the relationship that had not existed before. Perhaps the city child felt that they had left the country bumpkin far behind in the course of a year. Last year's girl companion had acquired new interests, and was no longer interested in catching frogs or fireflies. Often these constraints would disappear as you renewed your acquaintance. Both of you had changed and progressed, but these changes were not enough to alter the underlying friendship. Besides, you were stuck with each other, and isolation forced you to work through your uncertainties. Some friendships continued over a period of several years, ending only when the children grew older and found summer jobs back home which prevented them from returning to the lake with their vacationing parents. As I grew older, romantic interests developed, and these put to shame the frog-catching and all previous activities. Then we would sit on the dock on sunny days and talk and talk, and continue talking into the evenings until the mosquitoes drove you inside, and then we would crowd into a booth in the store and drink cokes and play the jukebox until our parents ordered us off to bed.

Our relationships with some of the adults who came to the resort were longer lasting and more profound. Ann and I were great favorites of our repeat guests who had watched us grow up year after year. Some of these were middle-aged childless couples who more or less adopted us to fill some emptiness in their own lives. Perhaps they saw us unattached, like orphan fawns, and wished to take us home. In at least one instance this was literally true. One evening I heard my father in a loud argument with a long-time friend and cabin owner across the lake. The gentlemen in question apparently felt sorry for us and wanted to take us home and make us part of his own family. The argument got hotter, grew louder, and father lost his temper, which ended the discussion. I suppose he was insulted that anyone would have the gall to ask for his children, even if the requestor had the best of intentions.

But this kind of affection for my sister and I was not uncommon. Many of our guests felt that way. It was like having a multitude of loving aunts and uncles around all summer. I spent many hours sitting on the dock with these people, cane poles across our laps, the floating dock gently rocking with the waves, engaging in hours of desultory conversation about almost everything. Small wonder we became close friends in a hurry. This was quality time which is almost impossible to have in the rush of ordinary life. Seldom indeed does a parent find time to hold such conversations with their own children. At any rate, we learned to love many of these people, and I believe they returned year after year to see Ann and I as much as for any other reason.

These people became our family and their annual visits were looked upon with anticipation. Their pleasure at seeing us after a year's absence was great for our self esteem, and we went all out to deserve and retain their respect. They did respect us—whether they were farmers or bank presidents—because we had some expertise that they needed. We knew where the fish were biting, and how to fillet their fish, and how to gap the sparkplugs on their outboard motors. We were their servants, but they were also our dependents, They needed us to provide them with minnows, ice, and outboard gas, and to help them bury their fish under sawdust atop the ice in our icehouse. In return for their dependency, we treated them like kings, which some of them pretended to be. Here, so far from home, they were able to recreate themselves into the people they desired to be. And who is to say that this joyful, playful, childlike nature they showed to us on these vacations was not the real them? Here at the lake they were no longer intimidated and powerless employees, henpecked husbands, hated neighbors held in contempt by their townspeople. Here, without time-clocks, without competition, without family pressures—they were a blank slate, and they could write on it what they wished. Ann and I no doubt heard their more outrageous claims, but we liked them anyway, and took them at face value.

Many of these people returned year after year until they literally died off. As I write this, I can recall at least one family who has come to the resort without fail for the last fifty years. Their daughter, who I rescued from drowning when she was five or six years old, also continues to return each year with her own family.

Not all the important (to me) summer people were our own guests. Some owned cabins nearby, or on the island across the lake from our resort. We called this island "John's Island" because an old bachelor by the name of John Nelson lived there when I was a child. John's only access to his home was by flat bottom boat in summer and by walking across the ice during the winter. There was a period in the fall during freeze-up when John was marooned there until the ice froze thick enough to walk on. He was similarly marooned in the spring. I recall John walking across the ice carrying a long pole to support him in the event the ice collapsed beneath him. This indeed did happen from time to time because of the current flowing through our bay when the dam was discharging water into the Sandy River. This section of the bay was treacherous whenever the dam was releasing water, and John's long pole was a prudent precaution. I remember his screams for help one day after an icy plunge, and the terror in those shouts stay with me yet. One day John failed to come for his mail for several days and father crossed the lake by boat to see if John had met with an accident. Father found the cabin without food, cold, and John dying in his bed.

Before this happened, John had leased one of the two cabins on his island to some railroad workers from Proctor. One of these people was a shy and quiet gentlemen who came to the cabin on weekends to read, and it was not long before each trip included several books for me. He was my version of the bookmobile before that concept had been conceived, and the topics of our conversations were naturally books. He introduced me to Clarence E. Mulford, the creator of the Hopalong Cassidy books, who still is one of my favorite writers of early western Americana. These books are collectors items today, and still very readable works. He also owned every Zane Grey novel ever written, and he doled them out to me each weekend like manna from heaven. I have often wondered whether I was just lucky to have access to these wonderful books, or if there is some spiritual connection between lovers of books that would find you wherever you happened to live. Certainly, every lover of books wants to share the particular joy the book gave with others, much as you feel obligated to share with others a spectacular sunset. Such sharing is a means of bridging the normal separation between people.

There was another island across the lake owned by a wonderful Indian women named Margaret Davis who had descended from Indian chiefs and had married one of the white workers on the Sandy Lake dam. Margaret was a wonderful athlete and long distance swimmer who had competed for a spot in one of the early Olympics. As a child I remember seeing her swimming far out on the lake, only her arms visible and rotating through the water like tiny propellers. Unusual athletic ability must have run in this family, which had also produced Ed Rogers, the great football All American who had played with Jim Thorpe at the Carlisle Indian School and later at the University of Minnesota. Unlike Margaret, Rogers was removed from his Indian mother's Sandy Lake home by his father at an early age and sent off to Carlisle to begin his education. Somewhere along the way Margaret also acquired an education and taught school for a time. She had several children by her white husband, all of whom were unusually bright, handsome, and stalwart people.

Margaret and at least one of her daughters moved to the Twin Cities after the war and ran a shelter for homeless or pregnant girls. From time to time one of her other children occupied the big frame house on the island, which had been built initially by George Snetsinger, an engineer who had built the Sandy Lake dam and other dams in northern Minnesota. George had married the Indian mother of Ed Rogers and Margaret after her two previous husbands had passed away.

When I was 12 or 13 the big house was occupied by her daughter, Jean, and her husband, Harold. I mention these two because they introduced me to Sunday afternoon baseball, which was one of the great joys in my life at that time. Harold played centerfield for the Sandy Lake team, and each Sunday he would pick me up and take me to the game which was played across the lake near Bell Horn Bay.

In those days every little town had a baseball team, and the competition between communities was fierce. These teams had some wonderful athletes, and it was not unheard of to attempt to import some snazzy pitcher from the city to pitch for the local team. But the local talent was usually quite sufficient to produce low scoring and very exciting games. There is no wonder that baseball was once the Great American Pastime. I can still vividly remember those sunny Sunday afternoons: the grand and classy-looking uniforms, the smell of newly-mowed grass, the chatter of the catcher, the thump of the ball as it whacked into the catcher's mitt, the crack of a ball meeting wood, the scramble to duck as a foul ball screamed by. The spectators sat on benches or lawn chairs at ground level practically on the foul line, so the danger of foul balls and flying bats and expectorated snoose was very real. Occasionally spectators were hurt, but none seriously as I recall. Occasionally a foul ball would dent the roof of a car, or break a windshield. And I can still see Jean Davis shedding tears on the ride home after husband Harold had struck out three times. And I also remember Jean's joy the day Harold hit a triple with bases loaded in the last of the ninth to win the game for our Sandy Lake team. To a young boy these Sunday afternoon games were the most exciting thing in the world, and they represent an era that is forever gone. The end of community baseball marked the end of community as we knew it. Because of the ball games, we knew our neighbors for miles around, and us children had real live heroes. Now the adults watch the children play rather than the other way around. The children may be better ballplayers as a result, but they have lost something too.

◆   ◆   ◆

In September of 1941 my father drove me to McGregor in his 1936 logging truck and enrolled me in first grade at the McGregor school. This must have been an auspicious or frightening day to me because I can still remember the day quite well. Father, after introducing me to the teacher whose name was Miss Lohgergrin, took the teacher aside and informed her that I had just lost my mother. The teacher thereafter took a special interest in me, which was no doubt my father's intention. He was also perhaps hoping that the teacher would take a special interest in him, but this was not to be. She did in fact take a special interest in me, perhaps because I was a good student, and often used me to help teach the slower children to read. Other children might have resented this, but I could wrestle as well as read, and do not recall any particular social problems with my classmates.

In McGregor at that time there were two grades to a class. The teacher spent half of her time teaching one grade, half of her time with the other. While one grade was being taught, the other grade was supposed to be studying the lesson they had just been given. However, I found it more interesting to listen in on the lessons being given the grade ahead. and found I could master those lessons too. I particularly enjoyed memorizing poetry assigned to the older students, and discovered that I had a love for poetry as well as a gift for memorization. This would not have happened to the extent it did if I had not been fortunate enough to have shared a classroom with older students. This was probably one of the unexpected benefits of the old one-room school. Second graders heard the lessons of the eighth grader as well as their own. The bright students could therefore progress to the limit of their understanding, rather than be bogged down at the learning level of the slowest student.

During school recess we went into the nearby forest where the older children built sophisticated dwellings using small aspen trees and twine. These dwellings became secret forts where the young builders met each day to plot additional mischief. Younger children like myself were not allowed inside. Looking back, some of these buildings were nearly as large as a garage, and well built. The ruins of these buildings still stood when we returned for the next school year, but interest in the dwellings had waned—either because all the young aspen had been cut down, or because the school principal had forbidden us to enter the woods.

Until the fifth or sixth grade we played tackle football during every recess. I used a tripping technique for bringing down the ball carrier which brought howls of rage from my playmates. They did not think tripping was fair, but I saw nothing wrong with the practice. I also spent a lot of time running with the ball myself, but don't recall other children using the tripping technique on me. These games were rough and tumble, but none of us got hurt until we were big and old enough to put on real football pads and helmets. Then, as a 118 pound ninth grader, I was forced to tackle 170 pound juniors or seniors. I found the tripping technique still worked, but I no longer used my leg to do it. Instead, I simply hurled my body into the churning feet of the ball carrier and hoped I was not killed. Some of the tackles made in this way were truly spectacular, with the tripped runner somersaulting 15 feet through the air before coming to earth. These tackles made me a temporary hero and won the respect of my bigger and older teammates, but each tackle rang my bell and felt like being kicked by a horse.

When I got older I tackled in the normal way, which was less painful but far from being fun. I must have grown wiser too because I no longer cared to be a hero. There was a wonderful linebacker playing in front of me who seldom let the ball carrier get to my halfback position. For this I was grateful because I found no pleasure in putting myself in harm's way. I did it because it was expected, and because I would rather risk a broken neck than have my friends think I lacked courage. Plus now I had a reputation to uphold. I had made reckless and daring tackles when I was too young and foolish to know better, and now—being older and stronger—how could I do less? You have to live up to your image. Few of us are brave enough to play the coward in front of friends and neighbors. Strangely enough, peer pressure today is almost always portrayed in a negative light, as though it can only lead one astray.

Our early philosophers and poets saw peer pressure in a quite different way—as a means to make us better and braver than we naturally were, to address our conscience in a profound way. Certainly, the poet was expressing this idea in those immortal lines: "the coward dies a thousand deaths, the brave man only once." This was certainly an idea dating back to the Greeks and the Romans and held by even primitive societies. It is an idea perhaps basic to the unperverted human soul. I say "unperverted" because psychologists in recent years have tried to do away with our innate sense of shame and replace it with self esteem. But this is obviously a fool's errand because how do you build high self esteem in a coward? The coward knows better even if the psychologist doesn't. High self esteem can only come from doing the right thing rather than the wrong thing. And what is the right thing? It is doing what community consensus expects and demands. In some instances, the very survival of the community may be at stake.

In the classic book, "Black Elk Speaks," the old Sioux warrior and medicine man tells of how the women of the tribe began a "tremulo" when their men went into battle. This was apparently a moan or a wailing designed to encourage the warriors to fight bravely and die if necessary. But the women were more than a rooting section. It was their job to remind the young men of their responsibility towards the older and weaker among them. and of the consequences—rape, death, enslavement—if the men failed to win. During battle, it was the job of the older men to continuously exhort the young men to not lose heart and be brave. This tells me that bravery and courage—even in a warrior society—are not the natural state of man, but learned behavior. One of our great problems today is absent parents who fail to teach their children the obligations of living in a civilized society. Even worse is promotion of the notion that there are no such obligations, that all such questions are relative to the individual.

These questions were not even a matter of debate when I was growing up back in the 1940's and '50s. A generation of young men had returned from war victorious and for many of them it was the highwater mark of their lives. This is not to say that they were all brave and honorable men themselves, but they expected such behavior of others, and most probably drilled it into their children.

As I mentioned earlier, the summer people brought joy and excitement into my life during June, July and August. School was the greatest pleasure of my life during the remainder of the year. School represented surcease from unpleasant and boring physical labor, a time to socialize with your friends. I dreaded weekends and the approach of the Christmas vacation because it meant work, and lots of it—shoveling a road somewhere, putting up the hundreds of blocks of ice needed to last through the summer, sawing up our winter firewood with a noisy circular saw into lengths short enough to fit the furnace. Father was one who believed that when you went to the trouble to saw wood, saw a lot of it—enough to last half the winter.

Getting ready to saw wood took a half a day. First, father would sharpen the saw, which was some three feet in diameter, by means of a hand file. Each point needed to be filed at the right angle, and each draw of the file across the blade made a dreadful screech, like chalk dragging across a blackboard. This awful screeching went on for an hour and was only a harbinger of worse noises to come. The saw itself was mounted on a steel shaft as thick as your arm which had a metal wheel in the center around which went a six-inch-wide leather belt which turned the saw. The opposite end of the belt went around the wheel of our truck which father jacked up so the wheel was not touching the ground. With one wheel jacked up, you could run the truck in gear and the wheel would turn while the truck remained stationary. The 20-foot-long belt which turned the saw was then put around the wheel of the truck, the clutch was let out, the wheel of the truck began to turn, which spun the circular saw at a terrific rate of speed. Needless to say, this operation created a howling chaos which has without doubt been adopted by the devil to torment souls in hell. Imagine if you will the rumble of the truck, the flapping of the belt as it went round and round, the high-pitched scream of the saw, the howling protest of the log as the teeth of the saw bit through it, the very ground shaking beneath you as you fed logs crosswise into the whirling blade which spun so fast that it was merely a blur. God help anyone who slipped and stuck an arm or a shoulder into the blade. This in fact happened often enough to keep one cautious.

For two or three days father and I would stand there, him feeding the saw, me grabbing the chunks of wood as they fell and stacking the wood in neat piles, all the time your ears ringing, your arms numb from the vibration of the log as the saw chewed its way through, your eyes reddened and sore from flying bits of sawdust.

At the time we poked fun at the Indians who only gathered enough wood each day to last the night, but I think there is something to be said for that point of view. Work should be fun. Cutting wood should be fun, and so it is if you leave off cutting before fatigue and boredom set in. Of course, when burning wood is a necessity rather than a hobby the game changes somewhat. The season becomes a stern taskmaster, and the prudent man gets his woodpile ready while he can.

Only school provided a release from these unpleasant labors. Education was literally an escape from bondage, and I quickly realized that in my father's philosophy there were only two acceptable activities: backbreaking work (there was no other kind that I knew of), or study. Study was the only legitimate excuse I found for not working, and even study would suffice as an excuse only so long. The real purpose of life was work. Not working in our household was The Great Satan, a matter of morals rather than choice. Refusing to work in the era I grew up was not an option. The sluggard was cast into hell, or at least into the street. And when all is said and done it was easier to work than not to, just as it is easier for soldiers to march into almost certain death rather than refuse. The forces behind you are greater and more certain than the dangers ahead.

4

THE SUMMER OF '46

I n the summer of 1946 when I was twelve years old my Uncle Hub was operating a training camp for boxers at his fishing resort on Lake Mille Lacs. There were some great fighters there too, and I mean world class—people destined to be champions or to fight the champion. The fighting Flanagan brothers from St Paul trained there, and also Jackie Graves, the great Austin featherweight who became my pal that wonderful summer of '46. Jackie was then 23 years old and soon to fight the legendary Willie Pep for the championship of the world. The sporting press had nicknamed Jackie the Austin Atom because of his size, his speed, his devastating right hand, and the fact that he came from the Minnesota town of Austin, which is where my Uncle Hub made his acquaintance. I simply called him: Pal.

Uncle Hub was my mother's brother and the youngest son of one George Clemmer who had settled his family on a prosperous farm near Austin and rapidly drank and gambled his way through a large inheritance from his father, a wealthy doctor who practiced medicine for many years in Cresco, Iowa. George Clemmer's sister fared somewhat better over the long run, marrying a man named Bert Dickey who went to Alaska during the gold rush of '98, became rich, and is reputed to have been the gentleman who—while snowbound in a blizzard with another argumentative sourdough—hung that awful moniker, "Mount McKinley" on the crown jewel of Denali Park. The name stuck, despite a hundred year battle to kill it.

By the time the Clemmer siblings were in their teens the family was already penniless and Grandmother Clemmer was taking in washing and cooking for railroad workers to support herself and her rapidly growing brood. Husband George disappears about this time, apparently exiting this world as a sequalae to heart trouble and one of his drinking bouts.

The Clemmar clan may have been destitute, but there was one asset they all had in abundance, and that was charm. They were also spellbinders with wonderful powers of persuasion which Hub in particular was always putting to profitable use. The Clemmer clan, almost without exception, were the warmest, most generous, most truly hospitable people I have ever met, These traits are probably not surprising since they were the direct descendents of people with two distinct (though not necessarily different) talents: medicine and cooking. The Clemmars were wonderful cooks, and the present generation continues to have doctors and chefs among its members.

The Clemmers were also dreamers with a romantic bent. My great-grandfather, the busy Iowa doctor, was no exception.

Doctor Clemmer raised blooded shorthorn cattle as a hobby, and one year made an old time cattle drive to Montana on horseback just for the hell of it. Perhaps doctor Clemmer dreamed of being a cowboy, but he tended to business first and—unlike his son, my grandfather—did not make dreams his master.

Of the present Clemmers—I speak here of my aunts and uncles—Hub was the promoter with the greatest successes, and also the worst failures. One such failed enterprise put him in federal prison for two years as a convicted bootlegger. However, the bootlegging rap did not seem to sabotage his future prospects, or result in any permanent disgrace. In those days, the bootlegger—at least in some circles—was seen as performing a public service.

Always one to share the credit, Hub did not do his prison time alone but took my Uncle Tom with him, and my father might have gone also, except that father was never caught, much to the chagrin of my two uncles.

While Hub was making his high quality hooch in Austin corn country, and Uncle Tom was driving the finished product to Cicero and other points south, my father was selling it over the counter in a gas station he owned on the outskirts of Austin. Behind the counter father had a deep pit lined with rocks. The gallon jugs of alcohol ringed the lip of the pit. In the event of a raid, it was father's plan to kick the bottles into the pit, where they would supposedly break upon the rocks, destroying the evidence. I do not know whether father ever needed to put his plan into action, but suspect he avoided arrest because he was more circumspect than his more flamboyant in-laws.

Both before and after his stretch in federal prison, Hub talked his way into at least part ownership of two or three of the finest restaurants in Austin, where he was a most talented chef, ably aided by the closely guarded culinary arts of Grandmother Clemmer who followed him from restaurant to restaurant for the rest of her long and blessed life. She cooked, washed dishes, was mother confessor to all the young waitresses, and worked literally like a dog well into her eighties. She was of French and Irish descent, quite tiny, witty, loved to joke, and simply oozed compassion. She could fuss over one in ways I have never experienced since. Upon seeing my sister and I after a long absence, she would practically weep at how "thin" we looked, how hard we must be working, how little we must be eating to be so starved looking, and on and on until we were practically weeping ourselves in self pity. Grandma Clemmer was the genuine article—a truly sweet and compassionate person who passed these traits onto her own children. My mother died before I really knew her, but I have been told that she possessed these traits in greater measure than all the Clemmer children. Grandmother Clemmer's only vice, so far as I knew, was her love for reading the most god awfully bloody true detective magazines.

In the summer of 1946, when father allowed my sister and I to visit my dead mother's relatives at Shore Acres, every single one of my Clemmer relatives were either living or visiting there. I was twelve years old, and embarking on the adventure of a lifetime. That summer I fell in love for the first time, suffered my first broken heart, and experienced the joy of living with an extended family. That summer I met famous people, saw violence done to those closest to me, and saw the wonderful potential of life stretching before me. It was then—and remains today—the most exciting summer of my life.

Shore Acres Resort in the summer of 1946 was an exciting place indeed. Not only were famous boxers training there, but Hub, who believed it to be his destiny to restore the Clemmer name and fortune, had surrounded himself that summer with almost everyone he knew and liked—friends, relatives, even others who just hung around living off his largesse. And it was not just Hub's generosity that kept people hanging around. Hub was the center of excitement, a whirlwind of energy, a man full of dreams and schemes which he was continually promoting. Uncle Tom and my father were immune to his promotions because of their bootlegging fiasco, but others were only too eager to be drawn in.

If Uncle Hub in 1946 was not quite rich, he managed to live as though he were. He drove the newest convertibles, had a new blonde wife of 23, dressed in fancy suits with a golden watch chain across his ample stomach, wore diamonds on each pinky, and took trips to Vegas and other then exotic places. He was also a shrewd businessman with an eye for the main chance.

But Hub was not the only interesting character to me—a boy of 12—that summer of '46. There was Hub's older brother, my Uncle Chauncey, a charming man who inherited my grandfather's weakness for strong drink. Chauncey was a dreamer and a voracious reader who lived a large part of his time in imaginary worlds. However, he was not a recluse but had the Clemmer love for people and liked to be the center of attention. He was a storyteller who could keep crowds of people enthralled with his tales, and they were tales. He was the most habitual and outrageous liar I have ever known. I doubt if he knew himself where truth ended and the lie began. This can be a real handicap when dealing with friends or relatives because they tend not to believe you even when telling the truth. This served to isolate Chauncey and perhaps made him feel more comfortable with strangers who would at least believe him initially.

Chauncey's other great failing was that he was a binge drinker who could not hold his liquor, which is somewhat of an understatement. During one such binge he ran all the customers out of Hub's classy Austin restaurant with a sword, perhaps thinking he was one of King Arthur's knights. In another incident he decided to go gunning for someone at Sandy Lake with a rifle, which my father had to wrestle away from him in a dangerous scuffle.

Outside of that, Chauncey was a prince of a fellow, generous to a fault, and a wonderful witty companion in a duck hunting camp. At the age of 40 or so, when I first knew him, he was divorced, owned nothing, and was captain of one of the fishing launches at Shore Acres, an occupation for which he was perfectly suited. He could play the expert, tell his tall tales, and exchange witty insults with his fisherman guests. To a young boy like myself, he was the incarnation of Long John Silver, a salty, charming rogue when not under the influence of demon rum. But when drunk, beware. Then he was obnoxious, unreliable, and even dangerous when in possession of the weapons which so fascinated him—medieval swords, pirate pistols, bowie knives as long as your forearm, and other firearms of all kinds. With such an arsenal at his disposal it was fortunate that he was a kindly soul who really had no desire to hurt anyone. To my knowledge, he never did. He was also astute enough in most instances to stay away from his family when drinking, and usually turned up sober when it was time for work.

I have often wondered what kind of a life Chauncey would have had if he had avoided strong drink. Certainly, it ruined his life in many respects. It destroyed his marriage, shortchanged the young lives of his two very talented children, and eventually shortened his life. But I suspect that Chauncey might have had difficulty living a conventional life even if he had not drank. He was an idealist, a dreamer, who perhaps preferred living in his imaginary worlds. Alcohol was of course the quick way in. He should have instead become a writer, which—like strong drink—would also have allowed him to be whatever he pleased: a medieval knight, a western gunfighter, a Great White Hunter on the African veldt, a trick shot artist in the troupe of Buffalo Bill.

My uncle Tom, who went to jail with Hub and was married—like my father—to a Clemmer sister, was cut from quite different cloth. Unlike Chauncey, in the Old West Tom might have been a real gunfighter. He had the eye, the nerve, the steady hand, and a killer instinct. On one trip to Cicero with a load of alcohol, Tom was driving and Chauncey was in the passenger seat with a shotgun across his lap to protect the car from hijackers or revenue agents. Somewhere in Iowa a car came up fast behind them, tailgated, and then pulled along side as though to force them off the road. Tom told Chauncey to shoot. Chauncey hesitated, fearful that the car held innocent people. Tom, one hand on the steering wheel, grabbed the shotgun and fired a round in the engine of the car alongside, which coughed, sputtered, and went into the ditch. Tom and Chauncey drove on, never knowing for certain whether their pursuers were revenue agents, other bootleggers defending their territory, or farmers out for a Sunday drive. If they were simply farm boys looking for a race, they must have got a huge surprise.

Tom's potential for violence always lay just beneath the surface. He had the palest, coldest, blue eyes I have ever seen, and when he turned those eyes on you in anger it was absolutely terrifying. In all the years I knew him he loved to drive fast, and could drive day and night, which no doubt made him admirably suited to running alcohol and staying a jump ahead of the revenue men.

One afternoon when he just barely escaped, his wife—my Aunt Donna—saved the day. Acting on a tip, the revenue agents were waiting at a farmhouse where Tom was about to arrive with a load of alcohol. Aunt Donna sat there quietly with the agents, biting her nails but also doing some thinking. When her younger, keener ears heard Tom's car in the distance, she slipped outside with the pretence of using the privy, waved Tom off, and closed the farm gate so that the agents could not immediately follow. Tom took off across country and escaped, but was soon captured and put on trial with Uncle Hub. At some point during the trial, Hub physically attacked the fed's chief witness and informer, a black man strangely enough, and the two of them wrestled on the courtroom floor before the astonished eyes of the judge.

Tom looked back on his two-year jail sentence as the best thing that ever happened to him. Tom entered jail packing 220 pounds on a 5 foot 7 inch frame. He was a crazy drunk who would clean out a bar just for fun, and was blacklisted by Hormel where he once worked. I have been told that Tom terrorized the town of Austin during his drinking days because of his habit of walking into a bar and sucker punching anyone who aroused his ire without warning. When Tom entered the front door of a bar, everyone in there, except perhaps the bartender, fled out the back door, scattering like quail at the approach of a fox.

After a short stay in Leavenworth prison, Tom and Hub were put on a surveying crew in the mountains of Idaho. Tom took to this wild, hard life like a duck to water. Hub, who was more fitted to bright lights and high living in the Las Vegas style, was less enthusiastic, and fell into despair.

They both returned to Austin when their time was served as wiser men, in the best physical shape of their lives. Tom dropped 50 pounds on those mountain trails, now weighing a trim 170 which never varied for the rest of his life. He never took another drink, and never missed a day of work until he had a heart bypass in his 60's and then he went back to work and died on the job a few months before he was due to retire.

Tom was without question my favorite uncle. He taught me and all my cousins to hunt and fish and bought me my first shotgun. He was a man of few words, but had perfect control over us boys. When he told us to do something we did it without question, which was due perhaps to our having complete confidence in what he told us, but also due to the dangerous potential we saw in him. Everyone I knew held him in the same awe, even though he seldom raised his voice. Children loved him. Adults still feared him a little, and showed him the greatest respect. And that respect was earned. Tom's word was absolutely reliable. In his actions he was stern but fair and just. You could trust him with your life.

One other Clemmer sister was staying at Shore Acres that summer of 1946. This was my Aunt Mary who was married to Uncle Ted, also of Austin. Mary was the oldest of the Clemmar children, a tall, shrewd and thrifty woman who had finished raising my mother after the Clemmer family fell on hard times. Mary and Ted bought a small store in Austin, saved their money, and now—only in their mid-forties, were retiring to a lake home on Lake Mille Lacs. They also owned homes in Austin and Florida. A childless couple, they doted on me and my sister and often came to visit us at Sandy Lake bearing fine gifts.

It must be obvious that if I were to arrange a cast of characters to spend summer vacation with as a 12 year old, I could hardly improve on the people mentioned, or the setting. But there was much more. This was the summer training camp of Jackie Graves, the famous boxer who would soon be arriving with his wife, trainers, and a retinue of real or pretended friends who typically hang around a world class fighter. All of us were excitedly awaiting their arrival.

Perhaps most exciting of all to me was the pleasure of living in the company of my slightly older Clemmer cousins. There was Sonny and Dick, both 15 and the sons of Hub and Chauncey. There was my cousin Jo Anne, then 13 or 14, the daughter of Aunt Donna and Uncle Tom. In addition to my cousins, there was also a tribe of young people from Austin who were working at the resort as dock hands and waitresses. To be in the company of these young people—all four or five years older than I—was an education and tremendously exciting. The days were spent swimming or fishing, the evenings in flirting and delightful conversation.

All of us boys slept in a dormitory room upstairs in the main lodge, directly above the dance floor. An attic passageway off our room led to a spot directly over the stage where a young and effeminate musician played the organ on weekdays when no full orchestra was scheduled. Directly above the organ was an opening in the ceiling where we hung our wet swimming suits, placed such that water would drip on the organist's head as he played. This must have enraged him, but he either felt outnumbered by my big and muscular cousins, or he never understood the source of the dripping water.

Our dormitory room above the dance floor was an exciting place in the evening, with the revels of the dancers wafting through the ceiling, and ghost stories continuing into the night. We were cozy and secure there, a pack of playful and mischievous pups frolicking deep in a den.

In addition to my cousins and their young male friends, there were also a number of young ladies staying just down the hall who were working at the resort as waitresses and cabin cleaners. A day or two after my arrival, one of the pretty young ladies of 15 or 16 took me in tow and let me share her bed while she took her afternoon nap. We kissed and cuddled and naturally I fell madly in love with her. But alas, she proved to be fickle and thereafter kept me at arm's length, preferring the courting of the older boys. I suffered anguish for several days until another prettier girl arrived at the resort and then I miraculously recovered. This new girl—a real beauty who was also older than I—was hotly pursued by the older boys, but chose me to be her companion—perhaps thinking I was a safer proposition. I learned something too from this episode—that the fastest way to forget an old love is to find a new one.

That summer vacation of 1946 at Shore Acres was thus a wonderful time to me, a time of joy and innocence that has never been duplicated. Nothing necessary to my happiness seemed to be lacking. Even Old Jim, a friend and former neighbor from Sandy Lake, was staying at Shore Acres that summer, and he was the only one who seemed to understand my broken heart.

Our morning routine at the resort seldom varied. I would saunter downstairs each morning and order a breakfast off the menu. Grandma

Clemmer was the cook, and she would come out of the kitchen and fuss over us for a moment, her poor little face worried and her voice trembling with concern about whether we had slept well, whether we were getting enough to eat to maintain our strength? Why did our faces look so wan and tired? And so on and so on.

Her saintly disposition only changed once during that vacation, and that was when I followed my older cousins to the roof and one of them dropped a large firecracker down the chimney. The explosion blew the chimney apart in the laundry room, scattering years of accumulated soot on grandmother's freshly washed sheets, and scaring her half to death. Then uncle Hub roared like a bull and reached for his belt while I made myself small in a corner while my older cousins took the brunt of his wrath. Grandma Clemmer's eyes flashed, but her worst epitaph was "dear me, dear me!" She wrung her hands in indecision for a moment, wiped her soot-covered brow looking for all the world like Al Jolson in blackface, and then came to my cousin's rescue and begged Hub not to shout at the boys any longer. The firecracker, she insisted, must have got down the chimney by accident, the damage to the laundry was really minimal, her morning's wasted effort on the laundry was no big deal, and so on in the same vein. Hub calmed down after a time, but us boys were still in hot water. The firecracker episode was the talk of my aunts and uncles for the next few days. I noticed, however, when the subject came up, that my uncles had to make the most concerted effort to look appropriately stern, and would occasionally start laughing in spite of themselves. My aunts, who knew what it was to have a washing ruined, took a sterner view of the matter.

This was undoubtedly a nasty prank, but it was a creative prank, and my aunts and uncles were perhaps proud to relate the story as an example of their nephew's creativity. Our punishment was to clean up the mess, but grandmother soon kicked us out of the room before we did any further damage.

Some of the exciting events taking place never came to the attention of our elders. With so many young people about, there were bound to be jealousies and rivalries in the name of love. One of the girls who worked at the resort—let's call her Phyllis—had a crush on the young organist. She fancied that another gal—call her Mary—was trying to cut in. Phyllis was better liked than Mary and had the support of our crowd, either because Phyllis had staked out her claim first, or because Phyllis was considered the weaker vessel and thus needed defending. Goodness knows none of us particularly liked the object of her affection.

At any rate, a group of us youngsters—including the disliked, boy-stealing Mary—were out for a walk one evening after dark. Perhaps Mary had been invited along so the other girls could straighten her out, or warn her off, as the case may be. The person selected to do the warning was none other then my love interest, Marge—a small, wiry, feisty creature who feared nothing. Mary was larger than Marge and was not intimidated by Marge's warnings to stay away from the organ man. Hot words ensued, and soon they were biting, scratching and rolling in the gravel road, their snarls filling the air like fighting tomcats. Little Marge finally rose from the dusty road victorious, though scratched and bruised, while defeated Mary stomped away in a huff, even more determined to move in on the hapless musician, who I am sure would have been horrified to know that two women had been fighting over the rights to his affection, when his tastes quite likely ran in other directions.

Us children, when speaking of the musician, referred to him as the "morphidite," which is obviously not the right word, or even a word, but it conveyed the meaning intended.

After this battle, I loved little Marge more than ever, respecting both her fighting ability and her willingness to do battle for the rights of a weaker friend. This fight was the talk and delight of our group for some days, until a more serious brawl pushed it into the background. In the days that followed, we spied on the musician as he sat sunning himself on his afternoons off with traitor Mary sitting in adoration at his feet, and I tried to get close enough to overhear their conversations, but they were wise to my intentions and would run me off when I got too close.

The next fight, which I shall call the "main event" to distinguish it from other minor skirmishes, happened on the 4th of July. A festive, circus atmosphere had prevailed at the resort all that week. The Dekalb Seed Company was holding its annual convention on the grounds at Shore Acres and a large circus tent had been erected to hold the revelers in case of rain. Uncle Hub was to cater the food for the several hundred attendees. This was a mammoth undertaking, and even us children were in the kitchen peeling sacks of potatoes all day prior to the big feast which was to take place on the 4th.

In addition to the tipsy conventioneers, there were scores of vacationers milling about, including fishermen, swimmers, and people on picnic. Down on the dock tourists were lining up for rides on the resort's two launches and Chris Craft speedboat. Firecrackers were exploding here and there, a precursor of the fireworks to come. The day was sunny and warm and the lake was calm, a perfect day for a holiday.

The trouble started when the skipper of one of Hub's launches failed to return to the dock with a boatload of people at the time expected. Everyone began to worry. The skipper was a young friend of the Clemmers from Austin who was relatively unfamiliar with the lake. There was fear that he may have experienced engine trouble, or struck one of the shallow reefs. Hub sent his redheaded son, nicknamed Sonny, in the speedboat to look for the missing launch. Sonny at the time was 16 years old, nearly six-foot tall and powerfully built, a fine athlete and undisputed leader of all the young men working at the resort that summer.

Sonny found the missing launch after a brief search and ordered it home. Impatient customers, he explained, were waiting on the dock for their own boat ride. The missing launch was neither off course or in trouble. The drunken party on board simply did not want their ride to come to an end. After delivering his message, Sonny returned to the dock in the faster speedboat and the launch reached shore about 20 minutes later.

I was on the dock when the launch returned. The men on board were apparently in a rage. I heard them muttering threats on how they were going to "get that redheaded guy." Seems he had splashed water on them when he had swung the speedboat alongside to deliver his message. Or so they said. But they were simply mean and looking for trouble.

Once I got the gist of their plans I sauntered into the crowd standing on the dock, and—once I was out of sight—bolted for the lodge to warn Hub. "They're after Sonny," I yelled, bursting into the barroom where Hub was tending bar. "They're after Sonny." Hub had no clue what I was talking about, but he followed me outside nevertheless, just in time to see one of the mob unload a haymaker on unsuspecting Sonny which knocked him flat. Hub, moving quickly for a portly man, vaulted over the steps and dropped the man who had dropped Sonny. My uncle Ted joined the fight and my cousin Dick. Sonny was back on his feet punching his way through the crowd like a red tornado. Then the entire parking area was a mass of milling, brawling bodies, people swinging, falling, getting up. The steps were crowded with shocked onlookers, most too shocked to even speak. To a 12-year-old, it was terribly exciting. Then, as suddenly as it all began, the brawl was over. The instigators of the fight simply disappeared. I don't remember seeing them leave. So far as I could see there were no definite winners or losers. My relatives had taken their lumps but no one was seriously hurt. Hub had a bruised arm which had swelled to twice its normal size. Uncle Ted had a badly swollen hand. My cousin Sonny, who had taken the first shot in this battle and was its first casualty, seemed none the worse for wear.

Hub reported the assault to the local sheriff, but no charges were ultimately filed. The villains were identified as habitual troublemakers from a nearby small town, and the brawl to them was probably no more than some 4th of July excitement.

To our family though, it was an unforgivable offense. To be attacked in a sneaky fashion on your own property was a violation of every sacred thing. For the next few days the fight was the only topic of discussion, particularly among my cousins who were fortunate enough to have participated. I hung around them as they rehashed every moment of the battle for hours on end. They remembered every punch they had thrown, and berated themselves for every punch not thrown—for opportunities missed: a chance to kick some bully in the head, to knee him in the throat, to kidney-punch him, eye-gouge him, Karate chop him—you get the picture. They were sure they would be able to inflict much more damage in any repeat encounter.

They groaned in disappointment that the boxer Jackie Graves and his fighting contingent from Austin—who were coming to Shore Acres in the next day or two—had not arrived in time for the fight. Jackie himself, or course, being a professional, was forbidden by law to engage in street fights. However, Jackie's handlers were both tough and willing. The bullies were fortunate indeed that these trained fighters from Austin were not on the scene that day, but the fact of their absence broke my cousins' heart. They were out for blood, and not enough had been shed.

All of this fight talk certainly had me primed for the arrival of Jackie Graves, the famous boxer from Austin who was the real thing, a professional who had fought and beaten most of the best. Jackie was 23 at the time and at the peak of his career, a handsome young man with a devastating punch. No fighter yet had stood up against it.

Jackie had pursued his amateur career through the honest and difficult route of Golden Gloves, winning the National Championship in 1941 as a featherweight. If not for the war, Jackie might have represented the United States in the 1944 Olympics, following the golden glove/Olympic career paths of other great professionals such as Cassius Clay and Sugar Ray Leanord.

Jackie was probably in his second or third year as a professional when I met him, and the top ranked featherweight challenger in the world, only one or two fights away from his bout with the then world champion, Willie Pep.

The Jackie I met in 1946 was a genuine hero, a true-life All American boy, and I was excited to meet him. My uncles had been priming both me and him for this meeting, and when the Great Man arrived he sat down and talked to me man to man, and generally encouraged me to hang around as his pal and listen in on his conversations with other well wishers. His trainers took time to thoroughly brief me on Jackie's rigorous training schedule—ten miles of roadwork every day, an hour or two punching away on the heavy bag, speed work on the smaller punching bag, jumping rope, several rounds of boxing with sparring partners, and whatever other tortures the trainer could dream up. Most fighters were much bigger men than their fighting weight would indicate, so "making the weight" prior to the fight was both critical and difficult to do. Some fighters gained forty or fifty pounds between fights, and suffered indeed during training. Jackie appeared to be nothing but bone and muscle already, though he did celebrate one evening with me by having a dish of ice cream, which I was told was a great indulgence.

I heard of Jackie in later years, when his career and the glory days were over, when his beautiful wife had left him, and he had been in and out of alcohol treatment centers. But the Jackie I see in my mind's eye is the clean-cut, ascetic young man of 1946 who sat eating ice cream on a summer evening surrounded by friends and followers, and who had the world at his fingertips.

A few years later Jackie's dreams of glory, riches, and world championship died on a similar summer night in a Miami Fight Garden under the devastating fists of Willie Pep, who has since been acknowledged as one of the great featherweight champions of all time. Jackie surprised Pep and nearly knocked him out in the first round, but Pep recovered and knocked out Jackie later in the fight. Jackie was never the same fighter after that. Never having known defeat, his belief in his invincibility was shattered for the first time, and it changed him. He had had the bad luck to have the great Willie Pep blocking his way to the world championship, for Jackie certainly would have defeated a lesser champion. But who knows? Perhaps a loss to the very best is superior to victory over the mediocre.

I saw Jackie for the last time at Uncle Hub's funeral in the late 1980's. He was a grey, quiet, unassuming little man who had come to pay his last respects to my uncle, or perhaps he was making a nostalgic trip to the past. Apparently he had stopped drinking and was living a quiet life in Austin, the glory days far behind him, still a hero to a few old timers who remembered, but many of these people dead or dying. At the funeral I did not speak to him or remind him that we once had been pals for a week in the summer of '46. Everyone had been his pal then, but all his friends—like me—had fallen away when the glory left him. Both him and I had lost something in the intervening years and I grieved for that loss even more than for my dead uncle, who had had to come to terms with the death of his own dreams a long time ago. But Hub had never been defeated. Even at the end of his life, when he lived alone in a mobile home working as a chef in another man's restaurant, he was still full of enthusiasm for the good life, relating to me his latest trip to Las Vegas, waxing eloquent over the night club acts and the beauty of the showgirls. The Clemmer ability to enthuse and energize others had not failed him, nor had he totally failed in his desire to restore the Clemmer family name. Though he died poor, with two failed marriages under his belt, one of his daughters became a doctor, continuing the Clemmer family medical tradition. Sonny, his only son, became a well known chef—as did Sonny's own son, Reed—so the family cooking tradition was also carried on through Hub's offspring.

At any rate, I have Hub to thank for my wonderful summer of '46, and I sometimes wonder if this was not the happiest summer for the entire Clemmer clan. This was still a time of hope and innocence, a world of peace after many years of war, The world, to me at least, was still a fine place, with real heroes in it. I was in a beautiful place, surrounded by friends and loving relatives. No wonder I see this time as a high point in all our lives, a period of bliss before reality and tragedy struck.

Because tragedy did indeed strike. The beautiful lodge at Shore Acres, with all its guns, mounted animals, and collected memorabilia of a lifetime, burned to the ground a year or two later with no loss of life but with the loss of every possession. Aunt Mary, my mother's oldest sister, lost her husband Ted to a sudden heart attack. Uncle Ted, having achieved his dream of early retirement while still in his forties, after a lifetime of scrimping and saving, now lay dead just after moving into a new retirement home on Lake Mille Lacs. Aunt Mary eventually remarried, but I do not believe that she was ever happy again.

So the halcyon days at Shore Acres ended forever. Hub left the resort and moved back to Austin and the restaurant business. His son Sonny married one of the resort workers and the two of them ran the resort for a time, but without the lodge the resort was a sad reminder of its former glory. Uncle Chauncey died alone in a Mille Lacs Lake cabin of a hemorrhaging ulcer and nobody around to help—the man who loved people and who had entertained hundreds, alone when he needed them. He was only in his fifties.

Aunt Donna and Uncle Tom bought a farm on a lake outside of Aitkin and returned to Shore Acres no more. Aunt Mary sold her retirement home on Lake Mille Lacs and returned to Austin, never to travel that far north again. No more fighters trained at Shore Acres and the crowds and excitement were replaced by silence and an occasional fisherman. A year or two after my visit, cousin Dick Clemmer was sent off against his will at age 17 to the Marine Corps, but refused to submit to discipline and spent much of his time in the brig. Dick was a man of tremendous charm and talent, but an unpredictable drinker like his father. He was also an inventor who took two businesses nationally before retiring to an island in a lake in the far north.

In the third week of my Shore Acres visit, father called Hub and ordered him to send me and my sister home. I had sent him a postcard relating the details of the July 4th brawl, and I believe father thought it high time to get sis and I out of that corrupting influence. It broke my heart to have to go home. After the wide expanses of Lake Mille Lacs, Sandy Lake seemed small, cramped and depressing. Home represented work, responsibility and loneliness. Gone were the good companions, loving relatives, famous personalities, and the magic that Hub and my Clemmer relatives were able to spin. Even today—looking back over 50 years—the summer of 1946 stands out as an island of joy and tranquility, where the world, to quote Matthew Arnold: "...seemed to lie before one like a land of dreams, so beautiful, so various, so new..."

5

COMING OF THE HIGHWAY

The following summer civilization crept north towards our little village in the form of a modern highway, and it changed the character of our previously isolated home forever.

During the early years of my life the highway ended a mile south of our home at Browns Point, site of the old Northwest Fur Trading Post. From there north a one-lane road skirted the edge of the lake and passed through Ridge Park Resort where one of the old Mississippi steamboats had been permanently docked to become a floating restaurant and nightclub. Nicknamed "the Ark" this 107-foot riverboat became a landmark in the area and a popular tourist destination. On a high ridge behind The Ark, the owners of Ridge Park Resort had built several cabins to accommodate tourists, all having a spectacular view of Big Sandy Lake. With the arrival of the highway, the cabin site was converted into a scenic overlook.

After passing through Ridge Park Resort, the road continued north past two or three private cabins and then rounded a sharp bend into the lakeshore town of Libby.

Our home and store sat on the north end of a high ridge which followed the west side of Sandy Lake. On the back side of this ridge, beyond sight of the house, father had built a large barn, which by this time was occupied by three or four cows and two horses, all that remained of our once large herd. Below the barn was a wet and nearly impenetrable swamp of spruce and willows, beyond which lay nothing but wilderness, through which meandered—in great oxbows—the Mississippi River. Near the barn was a large garden where deer came in summer, and on cold winter nights wolves howled in the swamp.

As I was growing up, the isolated setting of the barn was a place of terrors to me. Perhaps 10 years old at the time, it was my job to traverse the dark and lonely hill behind our house and milk our two or three remaining cows. This was no problem except on dark winter evenings and then this walk to the barn with my milk pail and flashlight became a gauntlet of terror.

My imagination was particularly vivid at the time. I had probably just listened to some tale of suspense and horror on the radio, and every nerve was stretched taut, my hair literally standing on end as I crossed over the hill and headed for the barn. The brooding oaks through which I passed cast dangerous shadows in the beam of the flashlight. Every moment I expected to hear the snarl of a lunging wolf, or the scream of a lynx as it dropped on my shoulders from a low-lying branch. I could feel its sharp fangs penetrating my neck, its claws raking the front of my coat in an attempt to get at the warm belly underneath.

Eventually I would arrive at the cold and silent barn, as black as the pit of Hades. A heavy door which hung on rollers on a metal track barred my way, and it was necessary to put down my milk pail and use both hands and all my weight to force the door open sufficiently wide to gain entry. In those few seconds it took me to open the door I was particularly vulnerable from some lunging attack from the rear. Nor was I reassured about what lay in wait inside. Shutting the door tightly behind me, I took a moment to direct the beam of my flashlight into the darkest corners. There was the rustling of rats scurrying for cover. I made my way to a single dingy light dangling on a long cord and switched it on. Now I could see the cows standing motionless in their stations. Some would low softly in greeting.

In the presence of the cows some of my fears vanished. But the wilderness that lapped at the very foot of the barn still swarmed with ravenous beasts of all kinds. Could they break in even though the door was shut? My ears were ever alert to the tinkle of breaking glass. Sliding in beside the cow with my stool and milk pail calmed me somewhat. So far I had remained safe. The cow was big and warm and comforting. Peace radiated from her as well as heat. I burrowed my head into her side and massaged her big Holstein teats until they were swollen with milk. Far off in the frozen silence I could hear ice cracking on the river, as sudden and loud as the report of a rifle. There were no wolves howling this night, but that meant nothing. They might be skulking in silence just beyond the door.

I milked the second cow, turned off the light, and made my way up the hill towards the house. The night terrors were upon me again, but it was better now because just over the hill lay light, warmth, and safety. Cresting the hill I could see the lights of our house. Almost there. But not yet out of danger. I glanced over my shoulder and hurried on. What a tragedy, I thought, if I were to be pulled down and devoured within sight of the house. But then I was through the door and safe at last. The house was well lighted and warm. George Burns and Gracie Allen were trading gibes on the radio. The audience was laughing. I switched the radio station to something spooky.

During the winter this scene of terror was repeated seven days a week. The fear of wolves was bedded in my very genes, perhaps the gift of my northern European ancestors who had feared wolves for a very good reason. European wolves had killed and eaten thousands of my ancestors over the centuries. One wolf in France killed over 50 people alone in the late 1800's. A Russian village had to be rescued by the army in the early 1900's when starving wolves came into the village killing watchdogs, livestock, and finally the villagers themselves. But North American wolves are for some reason different, not attacking humans unless rabid or otherwise sick. Some speculate that European wolves developed a taste for human flesh on the bloody battlefields of Napoleon and others who left the corpses of their luckless armies lying unburied where they fell.

Why had nobody told me in those days of terrified and superstitious youth that Minnesota wolves were pussycats? Would it have made any difference? Probably not. Even if the wolves had been proven tame, there were lynx about, and perhaps even cougar—any of which were quite capable of terrifying an imaginative boy. In truth, it was the dark I feared, the unknown, the mystery behind the silence, the icy touch of unexpected cold, the horror of dark water beneath the ice on the river. The radio—filled with tales of suspense and terrible, inexplicable happenings—undoubtedly fed these fears. Surrounded by city lights, I might have kept these tales in perspective. But here, living on the edge of a dark and silent abyss, all things were possible.

The coming of the road changed all this. Creeping up from the south, it swept away the cabins on the high hill behind the Ark and kept coming. It passed a few hundred feet to the west of our barn, isolating the barn from the mysterious swamp which had caused me so much anxiety. The road then continued north across a bed of fill before jumping the Sandy River, burying the most recent site of the Northwest Fur Trading Post along the river. Then it cut the Lockway homestead in two, separating his house—which had once served as the Libby post office during steamboat days—from the river peninsula where the town of Libby had once stood.

As the highway approached, Mr. Lockway got out his shotgun and threatened to kill any highway worker who stepped foot on his land. But to no avail. The sheriff came and disarmed Mr. Lockway and the highway crashed through his front yard, burying his garden and flower beds and destroying forever the privacy which had led him to buy this isolated place.

The road likewise torpedoed through the Bucholz farm five miles further north. This was one of the most beautiful river farms imaginable, with lovely fields along the river ringed by hardwood hills, with a trout stream flowing through green meadows bordered by majestic spruce and balsam. A showplace farm, which the highway cut in two as effectively as a butcher splitting the carcass of a steer. The coming of the road broke the owner's heart, and mine too, though I was but a child at the time.

I had reason to know the Bucholz farm well, for my father rented the place in the years just prior to the coming of the road. The property had a fine barn, where we kept our growing herd of cows, and during July we made hay on the meadows along the river. I first learned to drive on these meadows when father put me behind the wheel of our old logging truck, which during haying season doubled as a hay wagon. Initially, father pitched hay onto the back of the truck by hand, but now he had bought a hay loader—an evil looking contraption which would load the hay automatically. Automatic was not the same as easy. Equipped with wheels and designed to be pulled, the hay loader was a continuously moving bedspring festooned with large spikes which picked the hay off the ground and dumped it in the back of the truck. It dumped the hay so fast and furiously that someone had to be stand-ing on the back of the truck with a pitchfork to clear the hay away. Failure to clear the hay away would cause the hay loader to jam with tangled hay, which took a long time to untangle. Father could not clear the hay away and drive the truck too so he put me behind the wheel. I was only eight or nine years old at the time and could hardly reach the pedals. My job was to keep the truck astraddle the long rows of hay which we had raked into rows earlier. Since I could not see what was going on in the rear of truck, or hear over the noise of the truck, the hay loader would often jam despite father's most frantic efforts, and my only warning that something was amiss was when he leaped off the slowly moving truck and ran beside it, shaking his fist. I was excited about driving, but hated every minute of this operation.

On some of these same fields we also raised potatoes. My job was to ride and steer our horse, which was pulling a cultivator, down the long rows of potatoes while father stumbled along behind hanging onto the cultivator and trying to keep its blades in the ground and off the pota-toes. If the horse stepped on a plant, or took off across country because a bee had stung it, how father roared! I hated this job also, and have never ridden a horse since.

But I did love the Bucholz farm along the river before the highway destroyed it. The meadows where we once made hay have nearly disappeared now, overgrown with brush and encroaching aspen. The green meadow along the river, once ringed by stately balsam, has disappeared, choked by willow brush. The trout stream still flows through the missing meadow but one never sees it now as you cross it over a small bridge at 60 mph. A loved and nurtured piece of land in the midst of wilderness is beautiful indeed, an oasis in the forest where deer come for clover and sharptail grouse for grasshoppers. But now the land has returned to the wild and one would never guess what dreams had once forced it into bloom. I have the strongest memory of standing in the doorway of the Bucholz farmhouse and a kind lady coaxing me to take one of her fresh cinnamon rolls, still warm from the oven. The aroma emanating from that delectable offering lingers with me still, as vivid as yesterday. Vivid too is the remembered kindness of this wonderful lady who I never knew. In my mind's eye I see her as having passed away with the meadows along the river.

After severing the Bucholtz homestead, the new highway continued its inexorable march north, opening the wild country bit by bit to foreign invaders like ruptured skin allows in every kind of dangerous bacillus. The road's next contact with human habitation was the general store at Ball Bluff, which lay another five miles to the north. In the old days, a skinny and often impassible gravel road crossed the Libby dam on the Sandy River, continued north to the Bucholz residence, then turned east where it skirted Boot Lake, Blackhoof, and a number of other small lakes before turning west again to the Ball Bluff store. The new road cut the distance from our home at Libby to Ball Bluff by half, and cut the time of travel from one hour to 12 minutes.

From Ball Bluff the road pushed on, straight as a crow flies, slicing past the river town of Jacobson and continuing on to eventually meet Highway 2 at Swan River.

The last remaining wilderness in central Minnesota had now been breached, and my home country would never be as interesting again. There are more deer in the country now, and more wolves, but the country is not the one I remember. The mysterious and secret places have all disappeared, a victim of roads and the axe. My secret stand of giant yellow birch north of Aitkin Lake…those ridges of old growth pine, which I stumbled on accidently during deer season in the midst of a spruce swamp—all gone now, or breached with logging roads and stained with the exhaust of ATV's. Every secret place, hidden lake…clear cut, bulldozed over…pristine lakeshore sprouting wall-to-wall cabins as though some alien beast had abandoned a litter of ugly young.

But in the Spring of 1947 the coming of the highway seemed innocuous and even exciting. I could smell its approach before I saw it—black smoke from the fires of the woodcutters as they swept away the forest through which the road would go. When the area of clearcut reached our barn I walked the denuded hillside for a mile south, skirting the burning logpiles and closing my eyes against the smoke. It was quite exciting. For the first time I could see the mile-long ridge in its entirety—the view surprising and unexpected, and even shocking—as though some virtuous Victorian lady had been stripped of her clothes. The ridge had once had a fine stand of old growth pine. Where had they gone? What had happened to that old Indian trail that used to wind through the pines? I walked that trail several times each summer with my fishpole to try for sunfish on the shore of Bass Lake.

I continued on, past the smoldering brushpiles, the smell of woodsmoke mingled now with the sweet odor of disturbed earth, the emanations of 10,000-year-old humas ground underfoot by the metal cleats of bulldozers. Here and there lay the long, sinuous roots of Norway pine half in and half out of the sandy soil, the trees themselves flung kitty wampus into burning piles, or simply dragged full length and left lying to rot at the edge of the swamp. Giant stumps, uprooted by bulldozers, had been heaped in piles, soaked with gasoline, and set afire. After dark, the denuded hillside was aglow with these fires of burning celluose, the harvest of centuries exploding skyward in noisy sparks of flaming pitch. From my vantage point they might have been a hundred funeral pyres, a hundred Christian martyrs burning at stakes scattered about mad Nero's Roman gardens.

When I read in later years of the "scorched earth" policies of retreating armies, I knew exactly what the phrase meant. This denuded hillside behind our home was literally scorched black, and I can smell it burning to this very day.

Once the woodcutters and the fires had swept the ridge clean of every living thing, the giant earthmoving machines came, ridden by men who also appeared to be giants. The machines themselves had strange names which added to their mystique: TerraCobra, Turnapulls. Some had rubber tires 10-feet tall, and their riders sat higher still, giving the impression of men bouncing atop a Brontosaurus.

The mile-long ridge I speak of was a high one, and perhaps 70 feet of it needed to be stripped away and deposited in the willow swamp leading to the Sandy River. All summer long the giant machines rumbled by our barn carrying their gravelly loads towards the river. Nor did they move along at a crawl like bulldozers, but roared past at 30 miles an hour over the pitted terrain, their drivers bouncing in the saddle through the swirling dust like cowboys astride angry Brahma bulls. These men were heroes, sons of the Gods, and I watched them by the hour. How I wanted to join them on their wild ride! They were in fact modern day cowboys, intensely proud of their ability to steer a raging bull across dangerous and inhospitable terrain, swaggering when they walked, a bit of the showoff when they had an audience. Many were veterans, just returned from the war where they had driven tanks and dodged bullets. Their lives, for some unknown reason, had been spared while their comrades had fallen on the battlefields of North Africa, Italy and France. They were fatalistic, proud, surprised and happy to be alive, and felt themselves to a certain extent to be invulnerable. Most drank excessively. One of these warriors, who used me as a go-between to court my aunt (successfully, I might add) fought with General Patton all the way from Africa to Germany and was one of the few remaining survivors of his original outfit. His experience was not uncommon, but such experiences were life-changing and devastating for some. But for these survivors, gobbling up the landscape in wild machines gave them the power of gods, whereas previously they had been hapless victims of war. No wonder they loved this wild life and found it therapeutic.

Eventually the earth machines finished their work and moved north across the river. They had succeeded in rearranging earth that had lain fallow since dropped by the glacier 20,000 years before. Silence once again reigned behind our barn. The scarified slopes along the new highway were raked, planted with clover and jackpine, and the roadbed itself was allowed to settle.

During the next two or three years, the roadbed lay fallow while the roadworkers moved their operations further north. No traffic would be allowed on the new highway until it was completed all the way to Jacobson, some 20 miles to the north.

The coming of the highway marked the end of my childhood, the end of the wild country I had previously known, and it dramatically changed the lives of our family. Our resort and the town of Libby was now fenced in on all sides by highway, which deer, wolves, and my vivid imagination could no longer cross. We were not only fenced in but cut off. All traffic would now pass on the highway behind our barn, and the passing through customers would no longer stop at our store and gas pumps. Father decided that it would be necessary to move our store and post office to the new highway, which—when open—would provide the shortest route from Minneapolis to the iron range. It would be a busy highway, father believed, and so it became.

We began work on the new store the summer before the highway would officially open. The site chosen for the store was a level area to the north of our barn and perhaps 200 feet from the road. Father and I staked off the location one spring day and for the next month we hauled rocks and gravel to the building site for use in the cement slab foundation. We had no tractor or loader so this rock and gravel was loaded primarily by hand and hauled on the flatbed of our old Ford truck. The gravel would be shoveled—one shovelful at a time—into a small cement mixer, a little water and dry cement added, and the gooey mixture allowed to stir for a time, after which it would be hauled in a wheelbarrow and dumped into the wooden form which enclosed the foundation.

The foundation for the store was simply a solid slab of cement some two to three foot thick, and measuring perhaps 50 feet long by 30 feet wide. To fill this tremendous volume one shovelful at a time took most of the summer. To reduce the amount of cement needed, and to strengthen the slab, we filled the entire boxlike form with rocks before starting to pour the cement. The sloppy cement mixture would then run down between the rocks and harden, forming a solid aggregate that was practically indestructible. Professional builders, who used iron rods and woven wire to strengthen their own cement slabs, scoffed at father's method of using rocks for this purpose. But father never had a slab crack, and rocks were free for the picking.

For the next month I stood in front of our borrowed cement mixer and shoveled in gravel and cement, adding enough water to make the mixture sloppy. The tiny cement mixer was turned by an electric motor, the two connected by means of a belt, similar to the one that turns the cooling fan on your car. The creaking and clanging of the cement mixer as it labored under its heavy load became a familiar and comforting sound after a time, and I continued to hear it at night in my dreams.

Today, one could call up a cement plant on your cellular phone, order trucks sent out, and pour the slab of our store in a single day. We did it a tiny shovelful at a time. But time was something of which we had plenty, and the time spent did not seem excessive. It was equivalent to walking to town before the advent of roads and automobiles.

The walk itself was enjoyable, provided some healthy exercise, and allowed time for reflection.

Once the cement step was sufficiently hard to walk upon, father and my mother's youngest brother Ray—along with my own meager assistance—raised the 2 x 4 walls, set the roof rafters, and had the entire building enclosed before cold weather struck. By February the inside finishing was nearly complete. The sheet rocked walls had been taped and primed, and I had personally sanded and varnished all the doors and window trim. One of the final tasks was to sand the extensive wood floors upstairs in the family living quarters.

We were all elated. A long and difficult project was coming to an end. And we would meet our deadline of having the store ready for business by the time the highway officially opened in the spring.

A day or two earlier father had rented a power sander and sanded the wood floors. That same day I completed the building of an oak bookcase. That evening, before returning to our home on the lake for the night, father stoked up the new building's wood-fired furnace which delivered hot water to registers in each room. We took a last look around to admire our day's handiwork, locked the door, and stepped out into the night as we had a hundred times before.

That night a spring blizzard struck, the wind raged, visibility dropped to zero, and we all remained inside close to the fire. The next morning as we were having breakfast the telephone rang. It was our neighbor, the damtender, asking when our store had burned down. He had just returned from his morning walk to the Mississippi to read the water gauges and had noticed something strange as he walked by our store. It was no longer there.

We were stunned. Father sat at the head of the table with tears in his eyes, the first tears I had seen since my mother died so many years before. My aunt and uncle—who were to move into the new living quarters above the store in the next week or two—left the table in tears. I felt a twinge of grief for the loss of the bookcase I had just built, but the immensity of the tragedy was quite beyond me. We were all alive, and a store was only a store. But to my father and uncle it was the death of a dream, plus countless hours of labor. The grief and gloom at the table that morning was overwhelming, intolerable. I excused myself as soon as possible and caught the school bus to McGregor.

When I returned home from school that afternoon just before dark I saw a sight that I will never forget. There was father, all alone in the grey dusk, shoveling the still-hot ash and snow off the ruins of his beloved store. The wooden structure had burned completely, but the twisted water pipes still projected in the air in grotesque patterns, some with hot water radiators still adangle. All father's tools were also gone—hammers, skillsaws, levels, squares, table saws, sanders—tools which had hardly left our hands during the last six months. All gone.

I'll never know what went through father's mind that day as he shoveled the smoldering debris off the still-hot corpse of his store. He must have been stunned, discouraged, grieving. He could have got drunk, wept, railed at God, beat his family. Instead, that very morning of tragedy, he found a shovel that had not burned and started over. I was astounded, and fiercely proud. This, I thought, was the way to deal with adversity. Never give an inch. Pick up the shovel and start over.

When the neighbors came with plans to throw a benefit dance to raise money for our family, father told them, "thanks but no thanks."

Not that we couldn't have used the money. But we were not starving and the burned building had been minimally insured. A day or two after the fire the insurance man arrived with a check for $6000. It was woefully inadequate, but enough to order new tools and building supplies. In two weeks the debris had been cleared away and new 2 x 4 walls were going up. But now spring was on its way and the new highway would soon open. The new store would not be ready unless drastic steps were taken. Now we needed additional help.

Father hired a wonderful carpenter who lived nearby and we rushed the store to completion. It was built on the same foundation, but father changed the shape of the roof to facilitate the run-off of rainwater. The new store, in my opinion, was not built near as carefully as the old one. We were all in too much of a hurry, and weary of the project. But we completed it on time, and it became our family home for the next few years.

The cause of the fire was never determined. It took place without witnesses in isolation during the height of a blizzard. Had the power sanders used that day overloaded the electrical circuits? Or had the sanding dust floating in the air—said to very explosive—been ignited by a spark from the furnace? We never knew.

6

RICHARD THE LIONHEART

Richard was a son of the low hill country west of McGregor, very near where the hills sweep out of the vast bog which once had been Glacial Lake Aitkin. That ancient lake was almost totally gone now, except that across her willowy and flaccid bosom the Mississippi River still writhed and coiled like some undulating snake, impotent to either completely drain that ancient sea, or to call it back.

Richard's parents had settled on this mysterious highland, this island rising from the bog, and there ran a small herd of dairy cows for which they cut wild hay in season, and augmented their small income with some logging during the winter.

I met Richard for the first time in the fall of 1948 when he crossed the bog in a school bus driven by his uncle to begin seventh grade in the town of McGregor.

From almost the first day of Richard's arrival my friends began agitating for the two of us to wrestle. Neither of us needed much encouragement.

More than fifty years have passed since that day but I remember it all perfectly: the second-floor classroom where we discussed the arrangements, my friends gathered about with solemn faces and eager eyes, willing and ready to cheer me on, but for now wisely withholding comment.

I recall our silent descent down grey cement stairs, Richard and I in the lead, and the short journey outside to a patch of yellowing September grass just to the west of the McGregor school. I do not recall being particularly apprehensive. I had won such contests before and fully expected to win again. This was not a grudge match. Richard was simply a new boy in school who had to be challenged before we could accept him as a friend. Neither of us spoke as we faced each other. It was a sunny fall day, the leaves on the aspens and scrub oak across the football field just starting to take on their autumn colors. Richard stood subdued and looking vaguely unhappy, waiting for me to make the first move. I wonder now what thoughts were going through his mind as he stood there alone, a new boy among strangers, his status in the school perhaps hinging on this encounter. Was he fearful of losing? Or did he see this as an opportunity—a chance to knock off the leader of the 7th grade boys? Perhaps he was only regretting the need to humble me in front of my friends.

As I recall, any humbling was short-lived. There were no preliminaries, no circling to spot an opening. We simply stepped in and seized one another, each straining for a headlock and a rapid takedown. The next moment I found myself on the ground spitting soil and dead grass, locked in a grip that I could not overcome or even resist. Yet I sensed that he was applying only enough pressure to render me helpless, with vast reserves in store should I prove obstinate.

We arose from the ground friends. The silent crowd gathered about remained silent, either stunned or waiting to see how I would react to this defeat. I was in fact relieved. My temperament was not for fighting, and I knew that the mantle of champion had passed to someone more capable than I.

At our instigation, Richard soon got the opportunity to put his newly won championship to the test. The target was a bully in another class who we all feared and hated. He was a mean, ugly chap our age but a grade behind because he had flunked a grade, or perhaps more than one. A year earlier I had put on the boxing gloves with him but the match had been inconclusive. I was able to back away from his wild lunges, jabbing him in the face as he advanced, but I did him no damage and he never landed a punch on me. Fortunately, the lunch hour ended and we stopped boxing by mutual consent. Though I had not lost, I was intimidated; he frankly scared me to death.

I was thus delighted the day Richard agreed to take him on. We gathered at noon in a grassy corner of the school building, away from the prying eyes of our teachers. Just before the contest began, Richard did something that astounded us all. He offered to let the bully put any hold on him that he chose. This was the bully we all feared and Richard was giving him the advantage of first hold! We could not believe it! Nor could we understand it. The fellow deserved to be squashed. All of us would have stomped him if we dared.

The bully chose a full nelson from behind, both of them standing. The match commenced. Richard reached up, grabbed the bully's wrists, and simply removed the arms from around his neck. The act looked no more difficult than removing a scarf. Before the surprised bully could react, Richard seized him about the shoulders and slammed him to the ground, where he lay for a moment with bulging eyes before asking for mercy. As we congratulated our champion he was quiet and even looked somewhat ashamed, as though we had conned him into doing battle with an unworthy opponent.

Richard's next battle was unplanned. It was the first time I saw Richard fight in anger. All of us were roughhousing in the schoolyard when Richard found himself wrestling with an older boy who had a reputation for being both tough and mean. Richard had apparently got the better of the boy, for the boy rose in anger, seized a hard apple lying in the grass, and hurled the apple into Richard's face. Richard looked at the apple-thrower in surprise, and then, with a single blow to the forehead which landed just above the nose, he knocked the boy unconscious. Almost instantly, and somewhat miraculously, a purple lump erupted on the boy's forehead, increasing in size until it was almost as large as the thrown apple. We boys stared at that lump in morbid fascination. That day we learned that Richard had a punch.

And what a punch it was! One of my relatives had given me a set of boxing gloves which I had taken to school. It was common practice at noon to put on the gloves and spar with our classmates. These were friendly, bloodless affairs where nobody really got hurt. The exceptions were those who put on the gloves with Richard. And even Richard never intended to hurt. It was simply unavoidable. He had a devastating right which, if it landed,—and it always did on those foolish enough to stand and fight—caused a minor concussion. None of us put on the gloves with Richard more than once. This caused him much disappointment because he loved to box. In compensation, my classmates and I took it upon ourselves to find some gullible new boy or unsuspecting stranger willing to engage Richard in a friendly sparring match. Then we watched, not without guilt, as the lamb went to the lion.

One of these victims was a new boy from California who enrolled in McGregor as a freshman or sophomore. He was a tall, friendly, athletic, and very handsome young man who claimed to have had formal training as a boxer while attending school in California. He was a likeable young man who we had nothing against, though we had become a bit weary of his "trained boxer" claims. Under the circumstances it was inevitable that he and Richard would put on the gloves, and it was not long before it happened.

"Don't worry," the new chap said to Richard as we laced his gloves. "I'll take it easy. With my training, it wouldn't be fair for me to go all out." He flashed all of us a bright and confident smile.

Richard said nothing, only nodded politely. The California boy began dancing lightly on his toes, his left jab flicking out in the direction of Richard's chin. Richard feinted with his left hand and threw his looping right which caught the California boy alongside the jaw.

Never, so long as I live, will I forget the expression that came over the California boy's face when that blow landed. It was a mingling of surprise, shock, hurt, and perhaps sudden fear all mixed together. But what I remember most was his offended look, as though we—who he considered his friends—had betrayed him in some way, had set him up, had suckered him into something fearful and beyond his depth. He gave us a ghastly grin as his head cleared, but it was not quite a grin of defiance—more like the sickly grin of one about to be shot.

In the few remaining seconds of this contest the California boy looked to his footwork, dancing out of reach of Richard's devastating right hand, his footwork a thing of beauty and grace. Eventually Richard got close enough to hit him again in about the same spot on the jaw. The boy staggered and abruptly sat down, his eyes taking us in but unfocused, his head wagging from side to side in an effort to clear it.

I unlaced his gloves making a tremendous effort not to smile, not wanting to add insult to injury, or give the boy an excuse to direct his wrath at me. We could sympathize with his defeat, but agreed among ourselves that he had it coming. He had simply learned a lesson that the rest of us had learned earlier—namely, that nobody messed with Richard, even in fun.

The California boy returned to California at the end of that school year, never again mentioning his formal training as a boxer. But there was a change in him too. He never trusted any of us again.

I am not relating these rather harmless skirmishes to make a case for Richard as some aggressive and vicious fighter. He was nothing of the sort. On the contrary, he was a friendly and good natured chap who avoided trouble unless his own honor, or the honor of his class, was at stake. Then he was implacable and all business. In between these unavoidable unpleasantries, he was witty, had a great sense of the absurd, and was an interesting and loyal companion—a man's man if you will.

Richard's dream when he came to McGregor in the seventh grade was no different then the rest of us: he wanted to become a great athlete—to win glory on the basketball court or on the football field.

Nothing seemed more unlikely when I first met him. He was clumsy to a fault. It was quite obvious that he had never held a basketball before. He could not dribble, or make a layup, and was in fact so incredibly inept that we scoffed at his attempts behind his back. Me and the Ukura boy, on the other hand, were so proficient at basketball that we had been invited to play on the junior high team while only sixth graders.

We did not scoff for long. By our sophomore year Richard was starting as shooting guard on the varsity team, while my friend and I were warming the bench. Somehow, during those years between 7th and 10th grade, Richard had developed a deadly long-range shot and was a bruising rebounder, a talent which he came by quite naturally. By this time he had become a big-boned muscular youth just under six-feet tall whose strength and competitive nature made up for any lack of finesse.

But it was in football that Richard truly excelled. At the Letterman Awards Ceremony in his junior year, our coach—a college football star himself—characterized Richard as "the most vicious tackler he had ever seen—either in high school or college." None of his teammates considered this an exaggeration. We had felt the viselike grip of those powerful arms during practice, and with us—his friends—he took it easy. None of us belonged on the same field with him and we all knew it.

The secret of Richard's prowess on the football field was not immediately apparent to see him in his street clothes. There were larger boys on the team. Richard was, in fact, somewhat medium in size, weighing perhaps no more than 175 pounds. But that 175 pounds was all bone and muscle, and much of that muscle was in his legs. He had large, well articulated calves—a gift of nature and ordinary farm chores. How I envied those mighty calves! My own spindle shanks poked out of my football pants like the legs of a stork and I would have hid them if I could. Richard in his football togs looked every bit like a Norse warrior, those mighty legs as symbolic of his strength as Samson's locks.

Football was thus Richard's sport and he was as close as one could come to a one-man team. On defense, he played linebacker, just in front of me, and few ball carriers ever got as far as me. Richard made tackles all over the field with joy and reckless abandon, perhaps half the tackles made by our team in every game.

The most awesome tackle I ever saw him make was hardly even a tackle. Richard never left his feet. He simply stepped in front of an oncoming runner and took the full force of that charge directly in the chest. The runner stopped as abruptly as if he had run headlong into a tree. knocking himself silly.

On offense, Richard was just as deadly. He played fullback, and I played along side him as running back in the old T-formation. He was a devastating blocker as well as a tackler, blasting holes in the opponent's defense when it was my turn to carry the ball. I carried the ball with some success, but it was Richard who carried me with those devastating blocks.

We won our Homecoming game in our senior year by a wide margin. Richard ran wild that afternoon, scoring three touchdowns—one a spectacular 60 yard sweep around right end. I sprung him loose on that run with a flying block that wiped out all the would-be tacklers. Richard was not the fastest runner, but he was all alone when he reached the end zone. By that stage of the game nobody was particularly keen about tackling Richard. Those mighty legs delivered a head-rattling wallop to anyone who got in their way.

That night at our Homecoming dance Richard basked in the adulation of well wishers—a genuine hero and our Homecoming King, his dream of football glory realized at last, the most wonderful day of his life. We all danced or milled about the decorated auditorium until midnight, when the dance ended, and then many of us celebrated until dawn. Richard arrived home barely in time for the morning chores. That must have been a particularly satisfying moment for Richard—to see the sun rise on a new day after the most momentous 24 hours of his life.

He must have remembered that triumphant morning homecoming for another reason too. It was the last sunrise he was to see for nearly a year. It was the last time in his life that he walked from a car to his home.

◆   ◆   ◆

The fall of 1952 was the peak of the polio epidemic, and Richard came down with polio the day following the homecoming dance. It was a particularly virulent strain of paralytic polio known as the bulbar type, where the pharynx and larynx also undergo paralysis. Half of the patients who succumb to bulbar polio die immediately, unable to breathe.

The early symptoms of polio are headache, stiff neck and back, muscle pain and tenderness—some of the same symptoms one lives with as a result of the bruising sustained on the football field. Richard was in fact not feeling well the day of the big game and had all the symptoms of polio even as he ran for his touchdowns.

We students first heard of Richard's illness when we returned to school the following Monday. Richard was terribly ill, perhaps already dead. Unable to breathe, he had been rushed to Duluth and placed in an iron lung. His life—if he still survived—hung in the balance.

We were shocked but also philosophical. Polio was the scourge we all lived with. It struck unexpectedly and at random, like a wolf who one day pulls a particular sheep out of a flock. We grieved for Richard, but were likewise grateful that it had not been us.

Life went on. Our school cancelled the remainder of our football season and it was just as well. Without Richard, we were a lost cause. He was our heart and our courage, as well as our captain. None of us felt any more like playing football.

Another classmate, also in an iron lung, died after a short time, but Richard refused to die. At the time I could not understand why he chose to live, and it seems to me that he must have made such a choice. Life for him was obviously over. Death seemed preferable.

But perhaps I was seeing Richard's apparently hopeless position from the wrong perspective. He was, after all, young. And he had never yet lost a fight. At the time his atrophying body was locked away in a metal coffin beyond his range of vision. For all he knew, the battle had just begun, and victory was possible if not certain.

When we visited him during his year-long stay in the iron lung we naturally avoided any talk about his condition. Only his head emerged from that metal coffin and he looked quite normal, his face unchanged from what we remembered. He could speak quite normally so long as one of us stopped up the hole in his trachea with our thumb when he wanted to speak. It was a eerie sensation standing there beside him, the iron lung sighing with every respiration like the measured breathings of some sleeping behemoth, to feel Richard's words and syllables bumping under our thumb like minnows swimming down some flexible tube. The Erkkila boy, a tough football player, fainted dead away the first and only time he laid his thumb over those swimming syllables.

The day came when Richard finally emerged from that iron cocoon. In what could only be described as a metamorphosis, something had gone terribly wrong. There were neither wings nor legs on this butterfly. Richard was paralyzed from the neck down. He never walked again. He never moved again except for a right arm that became sufficiently flexible for him to feed himself. He never left his wheelchair except to sleep. Yet, despite this, he managed to climb the corporate ladder, buy a home in the suburbs, marry a beautiful woman, and father a son.

His family helped. His family helped in the way an artillery soldier aims a cannon. Richard became the cannon. He demanded that his family aim him at the targets he selected and his family aimed him. Talent, courage and his iron will did the rest.

It is a testimony to Richard's moral authority that he was able to command his family—particularly his mother and younger brothers—to wait on him to that extent. They did it out of love and duty, of course, but they also must have sensed that Richard—despite his ruined body—was still a formidable force, a cannon that only needed to be aimed.

I saw Richard a few times during later years when he came to our Sandy Lake resort from time to time to fish. His brothers would put him and his wheelchair into the boat each morning and lift him out at the end of the day. By means of a fishing rod holder and his useable right hand he was capable of reeling in a fighting pike. In the fall his brothers bundled him up against the cold and placed his wheelchair at the edge of a field or on a forest trail where a deer might come within range of his rifle.

During this same period Richard graduated from radio announcing school and became a disc jockey and commentator at a new radio station just starting near his home in Aitkin. He may well have been the station's first disc jockey. He was good at the job too, being articulate and with a fine sense of humor, his long illness leaving him with a wise and philosophic outlook. He remained living at home during this time.

However, Richard had greater ambitions than to remain a disc jockey in Aitkin County, as comfortable as such a position might be for a handicapped person. He finally resigned his position and moved to a Minneapolis suburb—again with his brother—and obtained a job as a telephone salesman in some small company. I suppose he was like a telemarketer, though this was long before telemarketing ever became a name in our lexicon. The next time I saw Richard he had become the National Sales Manager for this company, commanding a good salary and having hiring and firing authority. I suspect he was good at his work too, Despite his crippled body he still had a commanding moral presence, a near irresistible aura of authority. In his younger days it had been his great strength that had made him irresistible. Now it was his terrible weakness.

During these years I met Richard from time to time at gatherings of former classmates who had moved to the twin cities. As we became reacquainted after so many years, we began exchanging visits at each other's homes.

On one such visit he brought along a new bride—a truly beautiful young woman who had been married previously and had a young child. She had worked in the same office with Richard and over a course of time they had fallen in love. Now they had married, purchased a fine home in Bloomingham, and were living the prosperous life of scores of other successful career people.

I was astounded by all this, though perhaps I should not have been. How had he managed to acquire such a sweet and beautiful wife? How had he courted her? What courage it must have taken for Richard to propose marriage to this woman who must have been besieged by other suitors. And how courageous his wife had been to accept that proposal. Their union seemed so unlikely that I could only believe that God Himself had arranged this marriage.

We soon had another surprise. Richard's wife was pregnant with what proved to be a healthy son. How Richard must have rejoiced over this good fortune! To have succeeded despite every obstacle…to have made a career, to have become a father, to have achieved the American Dream in almost every respect that mattered. How had it been possible?

Richard did not long survive the birth of his son. That great heart gave out finally after 30 years of inactivity in a wheelchair. Like the salmon who dies after fighting its way upstream against overwhelming obstacles Richard had arrived at last at that quiet pool to which we all attain and delivered to posterity the next generation. How many of us achieve more?.

I often think of him now—that awkward schoolboy who came to McGregor in seventh grade and bested all of us in whatever sport we chose. How many times, with fear and trembling, did we send him forth alone to slay our school yard dragons? It is only now that I can appreciate how terribly alone he must have felt in those moments. The great irony here is that Richard was never a greater champion to all of us—and a more persuasive example—than when he had lost his physical powers entirely and was forced to do battle with every limb bound in the straitjacket of paralysis. He had been our hero before. Now we understood what heroism truly was. It was not about physical strength and fists but about heart. His lion's heart.

7

OLD JIM

Old Jim was my neighbor twice—once at the beginning of my life, and again near the end of his. He was my friend both times, though our relationship was obviously quite different at opposite ends of that 30-year span. Still, it was apparently always a special relationship, the kind commonly portrayed in stories about old men and young boys and the unique gifts each bring to the other's life. How fortunate the boy to have such an old man in his life—someone who can teach and encourage without reservation, leaving the discipline to others! And how fortunate the old man to get a second chance to be the right kind of father, after perhaps botching that role with his own children.

Old Jim was living with his family at a nearby resort when my father moved into the country in 1934. I am not sure when or how we became friends but it must have happened before I was old enough to remember. Since Jim was our neighbor, he was undoubtedly at our store almost daily to pick up his mail, so I suppose we got acquainted during those visits. But why we should have become friends is one of those mysteries that I cannot explain. Jim had sold his resort and moved to Minneapolis sometime during the war. There must have been at least a few years when we had no contact. Yet when we met again at Shore Acres in the summer of 1946 we met as old friends, delighted to see one another.

It is easy enough to explain Jim's appeal to a young boy like myself. He was the most charming of Irishmen, full of kindness, good humor, and wonderful stories. He was a pioneer—a wonderful outdoorsman who had been a logger, a market hunter, a resort operator and fishing guide—all occupations of burning interest to a country boy. Jim had no doubt kissed the Blarney Stone, but he was an honest man whose stories—though wonderfully told and exciting—were not blarney. He had truly seen a good deal of early life on the frontier.

Jim was a native of the Sandy Lake country, having grown up with several brothers on a small farm just to the north of our resort. Jim's father worked as a logger in the employ of Weyerhauser Company, which later bought large timber holdings in Washington State. The father died in a logging accident when Jim and his brothers were quite young, and Jim relates how the Weyerhauser foreman sent his grieving mother and her hungry brood a box of groceries in compensation. Perhaps a box of groceries was better than nothing, and more than the company was obligated to do in those days, but Jim recalled the event with some bitterness, particularly when he read in the newspaper from time to time of the Weyerhauser Company winning awards out west for enlightened management and good conservation practices. Jim maintained that the wealth of the company had been built on the dead or broken bodies of people like his father, and the theft of timber in Minnesota. Jim described in detail tricks used by the company to steal timber not their own, but that is not the subject of this chapter. Jim undoubtedly stole plenty of timber of his own. He was certainly an accomplished poacher. Hauled before the Aitkin judge once on a poaching charge, Jim appealed to the judge's sense of sympathy. "you're looking at a man who is down and out," Jim told the judge. The judge reportedly looked at Jim for a moment and replied: "You may be down, Jim, but you won't be out for 30 days." During those 30 days Jim's son ran the illegal muskrat trapline with no noticeable decrease in productivity.

I am uncertain of the ages of Jim and his brothers when their father suffered his fatal accident, but the boys were no doubt kicked from the nest quite young to look for work and help support the family. Jobs were scarce in those days and some personal creativity was often necessary to find work. One of the better paying jobs was fighting forest fires, and Jim reports that it was not uncommon to be paid to put out a fire that you had yourself started—a technique some experts believe is still practiced today.

With no jobs available and no prospects, Jim volunteered for the Great War sometime before 1918, suffered exposure to mustard gas in the trenches of France, and for the rest of his life received a small disability pension from the government. I never noticed that Jim ever exhibited any symptoms of being gassed. There were rumors about that some local politician with influence had obtained disability pensions for several of the local lads on their return from the war, so it is quite possible that Jim had not been gassed, nor even got close to the front. Jim never talked about it to me, and I was polite enough not to ask. I probably did not care to know the answer. But there is no question that Jim's trip to France expanded his horizons and helped make him the wise and perceptive gentlemen he turned out to be.

After renewing my acquaintance with Jim at Shore Acres in the summer of 1946, we continued to meet over the next few years when he came to our resort to rent a boat to fish the elusive bass of Aitkin Lake. He usually arrived with his brother—both rabid bass fishermen—and I was as excited about their bass fishing expeditions as if they were making an attempt on Everest. The Aitkin Lake bass had always had a certain mystique to me. I had never caught one, or even seen one caught there, but Jim assured me that the lake held bass—all big and extremely difficult to catch. Jim's tales of big bass were to me a siren song and I would have followed him anywhere for the prospect of catching one. Walleyes and northern pike—of which I had caught hundreds—I now held in contempt. Only an Aitkin Lake bass could satisfy that longing in my soul.

Jim and his brother caught a few of those Aitkin Lake bass on these summer trips, confirming their existence and firing my imagination even more. I dogged their footsteps from the moment they arrived at the resort, caught their boat when they returned from fishing, and questioned them fiercely about every strike. Being Irish, and wonderful storytellers, they were only too happy to oblige my curiosity. Indeed, my interest perhaps gave them as much pleasure as catching the fish itself. And I wonder now if this is not why old men and young boys need each other—the old men to conjure up memories that have lost their spice, and which can be recaptured through the uncynical eyes of the boy.

On those days when Old Jim's fishing expeditions met with success, I feasted my eyes on those mysterious and wonderful bass, poked their bellies, ran my fingers across their scales, hefted them in the air. These fish were all five pounds or more, their bulging bellies the deep gold color of the bog, their mouths large enough to swallow a man's clenched fist. I insisted on knowing every detail: What bait had the bass struck? Did they take the bait immediately as it hit the water, or on the way in? Did the bass jump out of water, and how many times? And so on. I was fortunate that Jim was a patient man for I certainly bent his ear with questions.

But all this information did not make me successful in catching one of these bass myself. And it was not because I failed to try or lacked opportunity. I regaled resort customers and my uncle Tom with stories of these mighty bass and connived to get them to take me fishing in Aitkin Lake. I fished the right spots with the right baits but caught nothing. The longer this went on the more obsessed and frustrated I became. I sent away for new and exotic baits, read all the books on bass fishing I could find, and still caught nothing. These bass were as elusive as the Loch Ness monster, and my frustrated fishing partners certainly must have doubted their existence.

On one of Jim's weekend fishing trips he mentioned to me that he was looking for a retirement home in the area and asked if I knew of any place that might be for sale? I pointed at the empty Stocker house next door to the resort and assured Jim that it must be for sale. I urged him to write the owner, a rich widow from Illinois who had purchased the house for her elderly, wastrel son in a futile effort to keep him out of the Las Vegas gambling halls. The son, who was used to action and bright lights, hated the loneliness of the place from the beginning—or perhaps he only hated this attempt by his mother to control him. At any rate, the son locked the door and disappeared one day, and some months later sent us an enthusiastic letter from California.

Without any real knowledge of whether the place might be for sale, I urged Jim to buy it with all the persuasive power at my command, and I had plenty of it in those days. I wanted Jim for a neighbor, and was not about to keep quiet until it happened.

It turned out that the owner was quite willing to sell, and Jim bought the house at a good price. I was ecstatic to have my friend next door, and Jim was ecstatic to have found a wonderful house perfectly located across the bay from the entrance to the Aitkin Lake channel and the bass and crappies of Aitkin Lake itself.

One weekend in August when I was perhaps a sophomore in high school, Jim bumped into one of our long time customers who had known Jim in the old days when Jim owned his resort. The two of them got to reminiscing about old times, and soon the talk turned to fishing and the wonderful crappies Jim used to catch years ago in Aitkin Lake. These crappie beds had lain dormant, unfished, and forgotten since Jim had left the resort some 15 years before. This conversation took place about four in the afternoon on a cool and overcast day, with me listening in. Jim agreed to guide his old friend to these forgotten crappie beds and the two of them set off for Aitkin Lake.

Needless to say, the two had wonderful fishing on these virgin fishing grounds and they returned to the dock well after dark that evening with a gunny sack bulging with 1-pound crappies. I begged Jim to take me there the next morning before our resort guests were up and about, the only time of the day I was free to go fishing. Jim agreed, and dawn found us quietly anchoring our boat at the edge of a weedbed in the farthest reaches of Aitkin Lake. We found the crappies biting as well as they had the night before. The bait did not seem to matter. Fishing with my flyrod, I caught them on minnows or grubs or artificial flies weighted down with lead shot. We pulled them in as fast as we could get our bait in the water, and soon had our limit of 15 crappies each. Even before this I had been casting covetous eyes at a wooded point some 40 yards away. This point was one of Jim's favorite bass spots and I was anxious to fish it. Before I could put that wish into words Jim said quietly: "We've caught enough crappies. Let's try for a bass."

I scrambled to pull the anchor and took the oars. A few quiet strokes took us within casting distance of the bulrushes and lily pads that ringed the point like some pendulous necklace. I had searched for frogs the night before in anticipation of this moment, and now I slipped a weedless hook through a frog's lips and tossed it as far back in the lily pads as the light bait would carry. On about the fourth cast the event that I had been waiting for so long finally happened. About halfway to the boat a large fish struck. "Do you think it's a bass?" I kept asking Jim as I played the fish. "It's a bass," Jim said confidently, though I know now that he could not have had a clue about what kind of fish I had on. I had been fooled many times before by dogfish and northern pike. In a moment I had the fish close enough to the boat for Jim to grab. He lifted it into the boat and I let out a yell. A bass, and a nice one. Four and a half pounds at least. Old Jim was grinning from ear to ear, relieved perhaps that this day had finally come. I was his prize pupil, and he was as proud as if I had won an Olympic medal.

We made a few more desultory casts but I was now anxious to get home and show off my fish. I was also late for work and worried about getting a scolding.

There was a crowd of people on our large floating dock when we arrived, not there to welcome us as it turned out, but all looking for Earnie Steele's minnow bucket which we had borrowed that morning thinking we would have it back before he missed it. Earnie was the friend Jim had taken fishing the night before, and now he had the whole camp in an uproar thinking some thief had run off with his minnow bucket.

Father was in a rage to find out that Jim and I were the minnow bucket thieves, but Jim took the blame, and when we displayed our fish he calmed down and said nothing. Dad knew good advertising when he saw it and this was classic: the young boy and the old man coming off the lake to a dockful of guests with a limit of fish, the likes of which most of these people had never seen before. How many customer hearts beat faster that morning as they stared with admiration and perhaps envy at that string of fish? How much hope and anticipation did those fish engender? It confirmed their choice of coming to Big Sandy Lake on their fishing vacation. Obviously the lake was full of big fish. Small matter if they caught none themselves. The fish were there and if they caught nothing they knew it was nobody's fault but their own. Fortunately, in those days, most people could and did catch fish. But nobody but me and old Jim could catch the big bass of Aitkin Lake.

That first bass caught that August morning with Old Jim broke the ice in some way and more and more Aitkin Lake bass began coming to my bait. But it was never easy or predictable. Like muskie fishing, patience and persistence were the key. Fishing in the right place with the right bait was important, but persistence was critical. You might fish your favorite spots 20 times and catch nothing, and on your 21st trip fortune would smile and you would lift your golden-bellied six pounder into the boat with pounding heart, your knuckles hurting where the reel handles rapped them as the bass took out line before those days when baitcasting reels had drags. A good strike was defined as one that most bruised your knuckles.

I suppose that today's professional fishermen could catch Aitkin Lake bass throughout the summer, but I could only catch them from mid-August to mid-September when they emerged from the rice beds and moved to the deeper bays where they wintered. The most productive times were during the wild rice harvest when dozens of ricing boats would ply the ricebeds and inadvertently drive the bass to the open water at the edge of the rice.

But this was not fishing for the faint hearted or easily discouraged. My uncle Tom, who was a dedicated bass fisherman, never caught a bass in Aitkin Lake in many years of fishing it, and finally refused to fish it at all. For him the lake was jinxed. Dozens of other people, inspired by my stories of big bass, fished the lake with me and never caught a single bass either. The lake, it seemed, was particular about those to whom it yielded up its bounty. There was no danger of the lake being fished out. The wild rice beds made most of the lake unfishable and the bass unreachable for most of the year.

Over the next few years I caught larger bass in Aitkin Lake, but none that gave me as much thrill as that first one caught under the tutelage of Old Jim on that August day in 1950.

Now that Jim owned a home next door we got to fish together more often, but he had not yet retired and I saw him only on occasional weekends during the summer. It was not until I graduated from high school and moved away to St Paul that my relationship with Old Jim developed further. He was living next door to the resort by now, and when I came home on a weekend I spent a good deal of my time at his house. If we were not hunting or fishing, we were about to go, or planning a strategy for the following day.

During these years I spent with Old Jim my parents were still busy at their resort next door. I felt terribly guilty watching them frantically running about waiting on resort guests while I sat in idleness in the home of Old Jim. I attempted to justify my behavior with the argument that I was earning my own living now, and had a right not to work weekends, but still I felt guilty and it caused some estrangement with my parents.

My friendship with Jim hurt my father for another reason. He had known Jim in the old days, just after Jim's wife had died during childbirth, leaving him in abject poverty with four young children to raise. Jim was unable to handle the grief of his wife's death and began to drink excessively. Some of his binges lasted days at a time. During these binges father took it upon himself to look in on Jim's children and occasionally brought them groceries to make certain the children had enough to eat. My father, who had lost (or was about to lose) his own wife, could not understand Jim's response to his wife's death. My father was a stoic, and Jim's emotional breakdown was totally incomprehensible to him. My father likewise could not understand why I should admire Old Jim to the extent that I did, apparently preferring his company to that of my own family. Of course, I never knew Jim in his drinking days, so I could only judge him on the basis of the sober, generous, warm and loving person he had become.

But I was not alone in admiring Jim in those years of his sobriety. His grown children loved and doted on him—despite the suffering and privation he must have put them through as children. His son-in-laws considered him the salt of the earth and could not do enough for him. They remodeled his house, added a porch, puttied the windows, and painted the entire dwelling without so much as Jim leaving his chair. Jim could get more work out of people with a word of praise and encouragement than others could get with a goad or a whip. Nor was I immune to his blandishments. I was happy to spend my day off doing work for Old Jim because he was so obviously grateful.

Jim was able to convey the idea that he desperately needed your help and that only you were talented and smart enough to pull the job off. With such confidence behind you, who could resist plunging into the task whether we knew what we were doing or not? If we were ignorant about the subject, we certainly tried to conceal it from Old Jim, though I suspect he knew our limitations well enough.

Outside of being an excellent woodsman and crack shot, I don't recall that Jim was particularly accomplished at anything. He was not a carpenter, a plumber, or skilled with tools. I never saw him so much as change the sparkplugs in his outboard motor, though I suppose he could have done so. The trouble was, nobody would let Jim do anything even if he had been so inclined. Almost everyone who hung about Jim's place was only too eager to jump in and do Jim's work before he ever had a chance to leave his chair. And this was not a one-sided exchange by any means. If Jim needed our help, we needed his approval for offering that help even more. Jim could see talents in each of us that we never knew existed. In his presence we believed ourselves brighter, more talented, and likable than we really were.

I realize now that Jim had that rare gift of genuine hospitality. If you showed up on his doorstep at 12:00 noon on Sunday (as I did more than once) just as he was sitting down to dinner with a tableful of guests, he would boom out a welcome, drag you inside, insist you take a place at the table, convince you that he had been expecting you all along—indeed, that the gathering would not be complete without your company, and that I had made his day by dropping in unexpectedly.

That I should have believed such utter nonsense is a testimony to the extreme egotism of youth, and also to Jim's powers of persuasion. But for all that, I do not think I would have been convinced of my welcome if Jim had not been sincere. I wonder now what Jim's sons and daughters thought as he dragged me to the dinner table? Did they resent this kind of special treatment? I never noticed if they did.

In the fall of the year Jim's daughters stayed home and his house became a hunting camp for the men. Duckboats were dragged out of the garage and repainted, decoys were restrung and missing anchors replaced,. temporary blinds were constructed in strategic places along the Aitkin Lake channel. Some of the most pleasant days of my life were spent there with Jim and our fall hunting companions. Jim's youngest son, Donald, was one of the weekend regulars. Don was in his late twenties and unmarried at the time. My friend, Jerry, who was to eventually marry one of Jim's daughters, was a regular visitor also, though Jerry was more interested in fishing bass than hunting ducks.

The life of our hunting gang was my uncle Chauncey, who I have mentioned earlier. Chauncey was one of the funniest men ever born, and we laughed at his lies, insults, and witticisms until tears ran down our face. Old Jim was Chauncey's hero also, and he hung around Jim and flattered him in the most shameless ways, all of which amused Jim greatly. Chauncey always insisted on hunting in Jim's blind—just the two of them—and I suspect it was because there were always dead ducks dropping in Jim's decoys. Chauncey was a terrible shot himself, but he could always depend on Jim's shooting to bring home a limit. If Jim was out of earshot, Chauncey would whisper in confidence that he had shot all of Jim's ducks as well as his own, and wasn't it a shame that Jim was getting too old to shoot straight? Jim would roar with laughter when we reported Chauncey's claim. On their next trip Jim left off shooting for a time, feigning gun trouble, and although Chauncey shot till his gun barrel smoked, hardly any ducks fell. Then Jim started shooting again and Chauncey miraculously regained his shooting eye.

In addition to being the camp jester, Chauncey—like all the Clemmers—was a wonderful cook. It became his role on weekends to prepare for each of us a duck dinner complete with all the trimmings. Navigating our way to Aitkin Lake in the dark, we would shoot our mallards, be in by ten to pluck and prepare our ducks for the oven, and then enjoy a most wonderful feast, topping off the afternoon with a nap, a Gopher game, or the world series on WCCO.

The smells and feelings of joy and contentment of these Indian Summer October afternoons are more vivid to me after 40 years than events that happened yesterday. This was a time before responsibility, a time of perfect freedom after years of bondage at the resort, doing those activities I loved to do best before they eventually became stale with repetition, surrounded by laughter, friendship, and good companions. These were the halcyon days of youth, and I know I was fortunate to have had the privilege to experience this joy of unencumbered youth even once, and to grow to young manhood in a time between wars and those horrors which have robbed so many of our young of their youth.

Those idyllic Fall days at Jim's cabin on the lake shaped my life and have a grip on me yet. A few years ago I had a very vivid dream where I was walking down a path through the woods to a strange and beautiful lake. I found my friend Jerry puttering on the beach as he often did, and when he saw me he said in an excited voice to someone standing nearby: "Hey Jim. Dave's here." The dream was so vivid that I mentioned it to a friend the next day and she put the same interpretation on it that I had. "Why Dave," she said. "You dreamed your own death."

It was pleasant to think so. I have long believed that heaven will be a perfected version of the place we loved best on earth. In my heaven I am certain there will be a lake, and drowsy autumn days, and clouds of waterfowl splashing into the wild rice beds.

These delightful days at Jim's hunting camp went on for two or three years and gradually faded away. I fell in love and got married. Jerry, my confirmed bachelor friend, married Jim's daughter, who we always believed to be a confirmed spinster. Both were in their thirties. Jim's son Don got married also—on the same day as my own wedding—and children soon arrived to all of us. I still spent time at Jim's house but the dynamics of our relationships had changed now that there were women and children involved. Little did we know that the gentle harness of responsibility was descending upon us almost without our being aware. My uncle Chauncey, who—to his credit—never took a drink at our hunting camp out of respect for Old Jim—went on one binge too many and died unexpectedly one night in a Lake Mille Lacs cabin of a perforated ulcer. With Chauncey's death went our wonderful cook and hunting companion and our hunting camp was never again the same.

My relationship with Old Jim changed permanently one Friday night in late fall when Jim's son Don and I arrived at Jim's house to spend the weekend. No one was home, and Jim's car was missing. There was no note on the table either, and this was truly unprecedented. Never before had Jim been absent without explanation on a Friday night when he knew we were coming. Where could he be? Don and I were worried, and imagined every kind of disastrous scenario except the right one. I had just bought some new leather boots which I was anxious to show off to Jim. I remember sitting in the porch in the darkness, waterproofing those boots, while Don was making multiple phonecalls in an attempt to track down his dad.

At some point during that long night Don did track him down, or at least discovered the explanation for Jim's absence. Jim had fallen off the wagon after a dozen years of sobriety. Nobody knew where he was except that he was in his second or third day of a continuous binge. Don and I were devastated—Don because he knew what his father was like when drunk—me because I did not know, and could not even imagine it.

Jim arrived home drunk the next day with some drunken stranger he had picked up somewhere and I hardly recognized him. His broken glasses hung askew on his nose, his voice slurred and hoarse, his eyes bleary red and crazy looking. I was shocked, horrified, and disgusted—all at the same time, and tried to hide it, but Jim was still sober enough to know my thoughts. As much as I tried to be compassionate, there was no doubt that the image of this man who I had so long loved and respected was shattered beyond repair. Jim knew it too. A long time later he said to me matter of factly: "You've never forgiven me, have you? I let you down." I made no effort to deny it, nor was he expecting a response.

In the two or three years that followed I did, of course, forgive Jim for falling off the wagon, but I could not forgive him for destroying my few remaining illusions. Jim had been my mentor, role model, and hero, and I believe that is what Jim meant. I had him on a pedestal, and when he fell he fell very far. Jim was not your ordinary drinker, but a souse—the kind you step over on ghetto sidewalks. His drinking bouts would go on for a week, during which time he never slept and never stopped drinking. He became as sodden and degraded as your stereotypical drunken Indian, whose company in fact Jim sought out during the course of his binges. How he found these Indian drinking companions I'll never know, but I assume he knew these people from his old drinking days, and knew where they lived. On one of these binges we found Jim's new Pontiac parked on the reservation, the car's upholstery stained with blood and vomit. Heaven only knows what happened there.

During the next three or four years that remained of Jim's life he was his old sober self most of the time. Perhaps twice a year he would go on a week-long binge, and these drinking bouts nearly killed him each time. Once he decided to sober up he would check himself into the Veterans Hospital in Minneapolis and spend at least a week under medical supervision while undergoing the horrors of withdrawal. He would return from the hospital subdued and wan, but he never made any promises of "never again." I believe Jim knew that now that he had let the alcohol devil loose it was stronger than he was. He could resist it for a time, but eventually his need or the temptation would become too strong to resist, and the cycle would repeat itself. During this period Jim's baritone voice changed to a whisper. The doctors could find no cause for this changed voice but Jim was positive he had throat cancer, and perhaps felt that death by drinking was a lesser evil than waiting for the cancer to kill him.

His family and I had many wonderful times with Old Jim after he returned to drinking, but the relationship had changed. Whereas Jim had once been a rock of dependability, he now became someone we needed to watch and take care of. We no longer trusted him. Did we dare leave him alone at the lake for a whole week? Jim needed company. Would he get drunk and smash up his car—or worse? Squander his retirement savings on his drunken acquaintances? Simply drop dead from abuse of his aging body?

For these repeated binges were taking their toll. Jim underwent more testing for his disappearing voice, but the doctors could still find nothing to account for it. Isolation and solitude—particularly during the winter—left him with too much time on his hands, and too much time to think. Between loneliness, worry over his health, and shame over his return to drinking—all these factors had perhaps robbed Jim of his desire to continue living.

Nor was I any longer available to help. By now I was married and living in Shakopee with wife, Katherine, and busy trying to raise two young children. His favorite daughter, Phyllis, who had married my friend Jerry, also had young children now and was unable to spend as many weekends with Jim as in the past. Jim's brothers too were starting to die off one by one and I suppose he felt more and more alone.

My last and perhaps most memorable adventure with Old Jim was totally unexpected. I had returned home to Sandy Lake for the weekend—I believe on a hunting trip with my family—and walked up to Jim's house about 7:00 in the evening to pay him a visit.

Jim was sober, looked good, and was in fine sprits. After visiting for a few minutes, Jim went to the cupboard and to my total amazement brought out a full bottle of whiskey and put it between us on the table. "I'd like you to have a drink with me," he said. "We have never had a drink together."

This was true. Up to this moment, in fact, I would have done everything in my power to keep Jim from taking a drink. I knew the consequences of his taking this first drink. At best, it would cost him a week in the hospital. At worst, it would kill him. But it was crystal clear to me in that moment that I could not refuse to have this drink with Old Jim. He was asking this as a personal favor to him, after all of the hundreds of favors he had done me over the past 20 years. This was no small favor either, because Jim had never asked such a thing of me before. He knew very well how I abhorred his drinking, and the disastrous baggage that went with it. All these thoughts flashed through my mind in the split second I had to make up my mind. Jim had never hesitated at any favor I had ever requested. I didn't hesitate either. Jim had something to say to me, and perhaps he guessed that this was his last chance to say it. Apparently he could not say what he needed to say without help of a drink. I could identify with that too.

Jim poured me half a waterglass full of whiskey, poured another for himself, and sat down across from me at the kitchen table where we had shared so many wonderful pot roasts and duck dinners. That table had always been crowded with guests and abuzz with noisy conversation, but tonight there was just Jim and me. We talked steady for the next three hours and it was like no conversation we had ever had. Our previous conversations over the past 15 years had been man and boy talks, the boy constantly chattering with persistent questions, the old man answering every question with patient good humor. This was the first man-to-man talk we had ever had.

Jim told me things about his life that night that he had probably never told a living soul. He told me about his wife's death in childbirth, and the trauma it had caused his youngest son, Don. Apparently, all of his children had favored Jim over their mother and accompanied Jim everywhere. Jim's wife felt neglected and lonely because of this obvious favoritism shown the father. When Don was born, Jim promised his wife that he would not become buddies with Don, but would leave him to his mother's care. It worked out as planned. Don became his mother's child, but then the mother died, leaving Don inconsolable, and Jim and the boy strangers. The father-son bonding that should have occurred earlier never happened, and perhaps could not happen once Jim chose to drown his sorrows in strong drink. Strangely enough, Jim was still grieving over this, believing he had shortchanged Don. He also must have felt some grief over his youngest son, Mike, whose birth had killed his wife. Mike had been given away to friendly neighbors when Jim's wife died. So many mistakes. So much pain. All of this grieved Jim now.

Jim had dealt with tragedy by turning to drink, unlike my father who had looked fate in the eye and said: "F...you." Two different approaches to life represented here, each with a different cost. Jim was the sentimental Irishman who loved too well perhaps, but was deeply loved in return, and was doomed to disappoint—because of his weakness—those who loved him the most. My father, on the other hand, would never betray a trust, but was too prickly to ever make his family totally comfortable in his presence. We dearly loved our father, but it was a love grounded in respect rather than camaraderie. His soft and tender side had died with my young mother, and he was, to paraphrase Hemingway, "strong in the broken places."

During my three-hour conversation with Jim that night we achieved a closeness we had never known before. The contents of the whiskey bottle diminished, but we were both thinking clearly and still articulate—the whiskey only serving to tear down the walls that men build between one another. We boldly spoke the things of the heart which we would never share in a sober moment.

At one point Jim apologized for destroying my illusions about him when I saw him drunk for the first time. "I could see it in your eyes," he said. "I knew you would never forgive me."

He told me he had loved me since I had been a little boy in my mother's arms, and this revelation did not embarrass me because I knew it must be true. Jim had been my friend before the age of conscious memory, so the bond between us had been established early. Jim had worked for my father in the woods, had shared meals with us on those days when they worked together, and no doubt was about our store a good deal when I was young. For whatever reason, I had become the son of his old age and both of our lives had been enriched as a result.

The only advice I remember him giving me that night was: "Don't ever become a bigshot." He didn't elaborate on what he meant by this, only repeated it several times. Perhaps he saw in me some naivety or innocence that he did not want me to lose. I think he was also referring to a sense of place. He was telling me never to abandon my love or sever my roots to this land where I was born. Outside of his stint in the Army and his dozen years of working in Minneapolis, Jim had spent his life here and his heart had always been here. He wanted it to be the same with me. He told me that night that he knew he had cancer despite the doctor's inability to find any cause for his disappearing voice. "I've had this voice for 70 years," he said. "I know what's wrong.".

I don't remember the aftermath of this last evening at Jim's kitchen table. I returned to the city with my family and I suppose he ended up once again in the detox center at Veterans Hospital.

The last time I saw Old Jim he lay dying of throat cancer in the cancer ward at that same hospital. We did not talk much that night because he was unable to speak and I was not in the mood. Besides, we had already had our talk across the kitchen table with a whiskey bottle and two water glasses as props. That had been the final act, and the goodbyes had been said. Jim was ready to go, and I was ready to let him.

At the end, we shook hands, our eyes met for a moment with that inexpressible sadness that one experiences at such times, and I walked out the door with a sense of relief. A chapter in my boyhood was over—perhaps had been over for some time—and I still had my connection with Old Jim's family through my bass fishing pal, Jerry, who was married to Jim's daughter. I also had my own family now, a new career, new friends, and my trips to Sandy Lake were becoming fewer. I was eager to begin a new phase of my life, certain I would never miss the old. But I was wrong.

8

THE LUCK OF THE IRISH

My chronicle of Old Jim would not be complete without my relating how my best friend and bass fishing partner came to court and finally marry Jim's tiny Irish daughter.

I mentioned Jerry in the last chapter as one of my regular companions at Old Jim's Sandy Lake home which we had gradually appropriated as our fall hunting and fishing camp. However, Jerry was such an interesting and original character that he deserves a chapter of his own. He was, for many years, my bosom companion, and our lives were inextricably linked for a dozen years.

Ours was an improbable friendship for Jerry was a dozen years older than I and a world traveler long before we met. He had spent a half dozen years in the U.S. Marine Corps as a paratrooper, and was one of those free-spirit adventurers who you read about in books climbing mountains, racing dogsleds to the North Pole, or doing other crazy and exciting stunts just for the joy of it. While in the marines, he spent his 30-day leave each summer fishing Lake of the Woods where he stayed with an elderly resort couple who had taken him in and treated him like their son.

It was part of Jerry's karma to be taken in and treated like a son wherever he went. He was the quintessential Irishman, friendly and outgoing, a lover of people, a happy vagabond. a wandering minstrel who carried his ukulele and his music wherever he went. He had a small and wiry frame, a ruddy complexion, and a thatch of tightly curling hair that leaned more to brown than red. He liked people of every station, but particularly favored ordinary people who did useful, productive work with their hands—loggers, commercial fishermen, carpenters, bricklayers—those who possessed some unique and useful knowledge that he could learn and incorporate into his own repertoire of skills. He was insatiably curious about everything, had the patience to be taught, the sincere and disarming personality which caused people to trust him with their secrets, and the energy to pitch in and do whatever job his host needed doing. Jerry was thus the perfect man to have around—a hired man who worked cheerfully for free, an interesting companion, an admiring and respectful student of whatever unique skill the host had to teach. Small wonder that strangers took him into their homes.

And besides this, there was the entertainment aspect. To poor and unlettered people Jerry was a book and television combined. At supper table, he would take his hosts to distant lands, from the South Sea islands to far-off Alaska.

He was the consummate storyteller with a marvelous eye for detail. He could describe the behavior of the Kodiak brown bear in a stream, of Arctic foxes robbing nests on the beach, of the migration habits of the red salmon—and all of this long before television cameras had invaded Alaskan shores and brought these images into every living room.

To the younger people in the household, Jerry brought his repertoire of old songs and his ukulele. He knew all the popular songs and the old ones too—all the wonderful nostalgic songs of World War I to the country songs of World War II including all the Glen Miller tunes. He could bang these out for an entire evening without repeating himself. When bumming his way around the country he needed to do nothing more than walk into a local pub with his ukulele and within an hour or two he was no longer a stranger in town.

Jerry seemed to be equally liked by both the men and the women. He was friendly towards women and always treated them in a non-threatening, brotherly way, but he preferred the company of men and cultivated their friendship first. As a result, the men trusted him. They also respected him. Jerry was a musician but no wimp. As a marine paratrooper, he had done all the dangerous things that brave men do, and he knew how to relate to potentially dangerous or violent men. Jerry was wise enough not to boast of his exploits, but in the course of an evening a hint dropped here and a story related there was enough to let his companions know that he had been through the wars himself and was not to be trifled with.

I first met Jerry when I was still in high school living at the resort. He stopped at the store one evening to obtain gas or water for his Model A Ford which he had completely restored and was driving across country from a marine base in Virginia to his annual fishing vacation on Lake of the Woods. I helped him check the vital fluids of the Model A and then we went into the store and visited for a time. He treated me as though he knew me, or wanted to—a personality trait that was part of his charm.

This brief visit stuck in my mind for some reason though I could not have explained why. Years later, when we became reacquainted, we both remembered that visit. I met a hundred strangers at the resort during the course of a summer and 99% of them I would not recognize if I saw them the next day. But I remembered Jerry. Perhaps in those few minutes we visited that evening I got a glimpse of the future and a world beyond the confines of Big Sandy Lake.

After this initial encounter with Jerry and his Model A, we did not meet again for perhaps five years, and then only by the greatest coincidence.

After graduating from high school I moved to St Paul to live with an aunt and uncle in the Merriam Park neighborhood, almost next door to where Jerry had grown up years before. This was a tough Irish-Catholic neighborhood which had produced the Flanagan brothers—Del and Glen—who had gone on to professional boxing fame and became world champions. Some younger members of this tough crowd used to come to our resort to fish (and mostly to drink) on opening weekend, and I met some of them again quite accidently after moving to St Paul.

One of these people who later become my friend and partner in a land-scaping business was still living next door to the home where Jerry and his younger brother Tom had grown up. He knew the family well and quickly briefed me on the exploits of both brothers.

Both Tom and Jerry were somewhat legendary characters in the community—Jerry because he was a fanatic and successful fisherman who brought home monstrous bass, and Tom because he could fight. In later years, Jerry had become the neighborhood's resident explorer and Great White Hunter. He had killed Kodiak bears and sent one of them home. Its head and hide covered an entire wall in the family rec-reation room. At the time of which I am speaking Jerry was operating a sawmill on Little Afognak Island off the coast of Alaska. He had bought the sawmill with the proceeds of a lucky commercial fishing trip. He and a friend had struck it rich, catching 6000 red salmon in a single day, which they sold on the market for a buck apiece—which was good money in those days. With the money, they bought an island and a sawmill, with a contract to deliver lumber to the salmon canner-ies. However, the salmon run failed the following year, and the canner-ies failed to buy Jerry's lumber. Jerry and his partner went broke, or got bored—perhaps both—and unbeknownst to anyone, Jerry was about to return home.

But before this happened, I met his younger brother, Tom. If Jerry was still remembered by some in his old Irish neighborhood, Tom was even better known because of his skill at using his fists. When some of the younger toughs spoke of fighters and fighting (which seemed to be a favorite subject) they spoke of Tom with awe. He was remembered as a tough kid in a tough neighborhood, a skilled boxer and street fighter who had both height and bulk to accompany his skill.

When I first met Tom in 1954 or '55 he had just returned home from a three-year stint in the Air Force and needed a temporary job. My business partner asked me to put him to work in our landscaping business. I must admit I was quite intimidated the day Tom showed up for work. I was only 18 years old, and here I was supposed to give orders to this mean and vicious street fighter. The job I had for him that day was to plant flowers. What if he was insulted and mopped up the street with me?

But I need not have worried. Tom was gentle and soft spoken, studiously polite and respectful. He could have passed for an ex-alter boy, which he might well have been. But noone should have been fooled. Just back from the rigors of paratrooper training he was in superb physical condition. And there was a steady look in his brown eyes that only a fool would misinterpret. He was quiet and gentle all right, but so is a leopard dozing in the sun.

One noon hour Tom took me to his parent's home for lunch. The family was now living in the Highland Park neighborhood of St Paul. Tom introduced me to his mother, a vigorous and gracious lady who spent much of her time these days doing charity work with the church. My business partner had referred to her on more than one occasion as a saint and I got the same impression myself. Not only had she managed to successfully raise three wild tough boys, but the patriarch of the family—the boy's father—was still a wild tough himself, quite willing to duke it out in the local pub after a few drinks. On occasion, the old man (also named Tom) would go out in his Highland Park yard late at night after a few drinks and loudly challenge his sleeping neighbors to step out and fight. Perhaps Old Tom felt guilty about abandoning his old Irish neighborhood, or perhaps he simply didn't like his neighbors, or perhaps he did it in the best of humor, hoping only to provoke one of the neighbors into some friendly fisticuffs. I am sure Old Tom's saintly wife was mortified by these nocturnal excursions, but old Tom—when not in his cups—was a gracious old gentlemen who reminded me of white-haired Thomas Mitchell in Gone With the Wind. I had been in young Tom's home only a short time before his mother began talking about Jerry. He was the eldest son, and she was obviously proud of him. Soon the pictures came out. There was Jerry standing with his chainsaw beside a giant Sitka spruce, with an Alaskan Husky at his side. They told me how Jerry had once brought or sent home an Alaskan husky which proceeded to kill every living thing in their Merriam Park neighborhood—cats, other dogs, along with chickens and geese which some of the neighbors still raised. If Tom had once terrorized the neighborhood, the dog was even worse and his sins less forgivable. His stay in St Paul was apparently a short one.

After the pictures, Tom took me downstairs to show me the recreation room. The recreation room was given over completely to Jerry's trophies—the Kodiak bear hide, a number of bass mounts—the largest over seven pounds—Jerry's custom-built 30-06 sporting rifle. This was the room where Jerry stayed whenever he returned home, and his presence here was palpable.

Why did this family who were practically strangers take the time to acquaint me with the life and times of their vagabond son and brother? They were proud of him of course, and perhaps I expressed interest. But I like to see this as providence at work. I was to play a pivotal role in Jerry's future, and the ground was being prepared. When he finally returned home he was not a stranger.

I met Jerry soon after his return home in the same manner as I had met Tom. He arrived back in St Paul broke, and my business partner sent him to me with instructions to put him to work. If ever a friendship was made in heaven, this one was. During his first day on the job the gas line on my powermower broke. Jerry repaired the break with a piece of string, and repaired it so well that I used the lawnmower for the rest of the summer without bothering to replace the gas line. At the end of his second day on the job—I believe it was now Friday—we were heading north to fish bass on Aitkin Lake. By this time we were fast friends, and for the next dozen years there was hardly a weekend we did not spend together fishing, hunting, playing guitars, and—after we were both married—with each other's families.

For a long time Jerry was my friend, companion, and mentor. Being a dozen years older than me, he had much to teach me that was both useful and fascinating. His range of interests and talents were amazing to me and often surprising. I was learning to play the guitar at the time and began plinking away on one of our early fishing trips. Jerry listened for a moment, and then took the guitar from me and taught me to play the Steel Guitar Rag, a song that he had learned by rote from some southern hillbillies while in the Marines.

Jerry read no music, but he never forgot a song he had once learned, and he taught them to me—undoubtedly with a few notes missing which I was eventually able to fill in. Besides the guitar, he had also taught himself to play the ukulele and the piano in the honky tonk style of Floyd Craemer.

While I eventually surpassed Jerry in technical skills on the guitar, I never surpassed him in making music. He had music in his very soul, and when he started to play his ukulele, everyone within earshot began to tap their foot, and sing along. During the long summer afternoons, between our early morning and late evening fishing excursions, we would sit on hard wooden chairs in front of Old Jim's cabin and play by the hour for whoever wanted to listen. Our resort was just next door, so we always had an audience.

We were a good pair—despite the difference in our ages—the melancholy Dane and the outgoing, exuberant Irishman. He had a zest for life and adventuresome spirit that energized me. I, in turn, had an analytical side which brought some science and planning into our activities. I read all the bass fishing books, and our fishing strategies were as much discussed and as carefully executed as any military campaign. But all this planning—while great fun—did not contribute noticeably to our success if the bass themselves chose not to participate. We tried fishing deep water, and sunken weed beds, but never had luck until the bass left their wild rice jungle and moved into the lily pads at the edge of deep water.

On one of our first fishing trips to Sandy, I introduced Jerry to Old Jim, and these two proud Irishmen—veterans of two different wars—were totally smitten with each other. From that day on, we were a fishing threesome with Jim guiding and acquainting us with the history of the area. Jerry and Jim made a wonderful team in another way. As I mentioned, Jerry loved to work with his hands, and Jim—with an old home to modernize—found ways to put Jerry's hands to work. But at Jim's home, fishing always came before work, and any work Jerry did for Old Jim was a labor of love.

On one of those summer weekends Jim's unmarried daughter, Phyllis, showed up at Jim's lake home with two or three girlfriends. Phyllis was a wee Irish lass in her early thirties. Jerry and I entertained the ladies with guitars and ukuleles when we were not fishing. I had no interest in these ladies, who were much older than I, and believed—somewhat naively—that Jerry had no interest either. Imagine my surprise when he told me one day that he and Phyllis were engaged to be married. I had not so much as noticed a suggestive look pass between them.

But we all agreed that it was a wonderful match—the wiry Irish bachelor and the tiny Irish spinster—finding each other at this stage of their lives. Phyllis was the apple of Old Jim's eye – they had shared an apartment together in Minneapolis for many years—and Jim was delighted that Phyllis had found a good husband. In truth, Jim could not have found a more suitable son-in-law if he had ordered him to specification. Jerry loved Old Jim as well as the daughter. He was the right religion and ethnic background, enjoyed the right hobbies, had masonry skills that Jim could put to use in restoring his retirement home, and was an ardent sportsman who would take Jim fishing for as long as Jim had strength to hold a fishpole. Jim was about to retire, and this must have been one of the happiest periods of his life.

Jerry's marriage did not affect our friendship at all. I was also married by this time and our two families spent much time together, both at the lake and at Jerry's home in St Paul. He had indeed, for the first time in his wandering life, put down permanent roots. With his veteran's preference, he got a civil service job at Fort Snelling, maintaining the old buildings there and doing whatever needed doing: painting, cement work, plastering walls. This was a job that suited him. At the same time he bought his old family home in St Paul and was soon busy restoring the home's beautiful oak woodwork and cabinets that had been painted over by previous occupants. In his spare time, he furnished the home with magnificent oak furniture he found at various estate sales and refinished. In two or three years this old home became a showplace thanks to Jerry's marvelous craftsmanship.

My wife Kathy and I spent many Saturday nights in Jerry's St. Paul home. He usually had something new to show me—a refinished oak commode, a table, restored birch cupboards in the kitchen. In the evenings, after dinner and a drink or two, Jerry and I would retire to the parlor where he would play old and nostalgic songs on the piano. Sitting there in the parlor, with Jerry playing the piano, the children playing nearby, and Kathy and Phyllis visiting quietly in the kitchen, I invariably experienced a profound and inexplicable sadness, as though I realized that this was as good as life got, and that it could not last. Perhaps this was simply the innate melancholy of the Dane, or perhaps I already had premonitions of tragedy to come. But sadness and separation were still far in the future. Most of the years Jerry and I shared together were full of joy and excitement. There were exciting and productive fishing trips to Lake of the Woods, where we portaged up unnamed streams to near virgin lakes on the Alneau Peninsula which jutted into the eastern side of Lake of the Woods like a clenched fist. We carried canoes and bags of decoys into remote lakes in the Big Sandy area where we had wonderful mallard shooting. And in November we walked miles in the wild country north of Aitkin Lake pursuing deer.

But Jerry's greatest love was fishing, particularly bass fishing. He had caught many big bass, as the trophies in his game room attested, but he was still looking for the "big one"—eight, nine, or ten pounds—and he was convinced that such a trophy still swam in Aitkin Lake. Indeed, Old Jim told us of an 8 pounder caught by accident by an Iowa farmer. Jerry's interest had been piqued by these stories, but in our first two or three trips to the lake we had caught nothing and he was not impressed. He went so far as to state that any bass caught in Aitkin Lake was simply a fluke, too few in number to seriously pursue.

Then one day something happened which changed his opinion. It was Opening Day of duck season and Jerry and I and my Uncle Tom had gone to Aitkin Lake in Tom's boat to hunt ducks. Jerry was not really interested in duck hunting, but he had bought himself a shotgun and started hunting mainly as a favor to me and Old Jim. On this particular day we were guests of my Uncle Tom, who was an avid duck hunter, and we had taken our fishing rods along to kill time until the duck season opened at noon.

We pulled into the point where I had caught my first bass with Old Jim and started casting, Jerry throwing a Shakespeare mouse. On Jerry's third or fourth cast, he hooked and landed a six pounder. A few minutes later he caught another just as large. By this time Jerry was literally foaming at the mouth. Uncle Tom's eyes were bulging, perhaps with envy, for he himself had never caught an Aitkin Lake bass. I was overjoyed to finally have my tales of big bass vindicated. It was quite obvious that the Aitkin Lake bass were on one of their rare feeding sprees, and today was the day to catch that trophy of a lifetime.

Alas. Uncle Tom insisted we go to shore and pick out a duckhunting blind before all the choice spots were taken. It was by now perhaps ten in the morning, and we still had two hours to wait before the season opened.

And wait we did. Tom oared us back into a weedy bay and there we sat for the next two hours waiting for the season to open. Once the season opened, we continued to sit there for the next five hours waiting for the ducks to fly. They never did. But we could see the swirls and whirls of big bass ferociously feeding in the shallows only a stone's throw away. Jerry was fit to be tied. This was equivalent to sitting him down before a feast but not allowing him to eat. He never forgave Tom for making him sit there, and if he ever mentioned Tom's name again it was invariably juxtapositioned with a curse, "that SOB Tom…" And from that day on Jerry never again put himself in a position where he was not the captain of his own ship so to speak.

The next weekend Jerry had to stay home tending to responsibilities in the city. He insisted, however, that I go bass fishing to see if our previous weekend's catch had been just a fluke. But they were still biting. I went alone on an overcast morning and caught one large bass and lost another because I was not paying attention. Someone shot at a duck behind me at the precise moment my Johnson spoon was hitting the water. I turned to see what the hunter was shooting at when the bass struck, almost tearing the rod from my hand. It was the hardest bass strike I ever had, save one.

I called Jerry and informed me of the results of my solo fishing adventure. He was finally convinced. The Aitkin Lake bass were for real. From that day on he and I pursued them at every opportunity. The two big bass he caught fishing with Uncle Tom the week previously took their place on his wall along with the others. But the Aitkin Lake bass, with their deep golden bellies, were the most beautiful bass of them all.

Jerry got another opportunity at October bass on a feeding spree a few years later. By this time he absolutely refused to hunt ducks when he could be fishing. Once again it was the opening day of duck season. Jerry went fishing alone. My wife and I chose to go duck hunting on a nearby slough. When we returned home later that evening we found Jerry sitting in our store with a wide grin on his face and a washtub full of big bass. He had kept six—all four, five, and six pounders. It was the most magnificent string of bass I have ever witnessed.

Jerry soon filled us in on the details. The bass were schooled up along a deep sand shore on an island that some duck hunter had staked out for placing his decoys. This complicated Jerry's task because the bass were very near the decoys. Jerry knew that he could not continually fish in the man's decoys without having a fight on his hands, so he worked his way up and down the shore of the island, each approach to the decoys producing a bass or two. The hunter never saw him catch a bass. Each time he had one on he would quietly guide it to the side of the boat opposite the hunter and quickly snake it over the side when the hunter was looking off in another direction. I imagine that the puzzled and perhaps angry hunter wondered why in hell this fisherman insisted on fishing in the shadow of his decoys.

This was undoubtedly the high point of Jerry's bass fishing experience on Aitkin Lake. I was sorry to have missed it, but my own moment of glory came a year or two later.

It happened like this. Jerry and I had been harvesting wild rice for the previous two weeks and the rice was well picked over. There was a pothole off the Aitkin Lake channel which we had not yet tried, so we decided to portage in there, taking our fishpoles along in case there was no rice to be found. We had never caught a bass in this particular pothole, but thought it worth a cast or two as long as we were in there. The little lake was not easy to reach and well away from our usual fishing spots—not a place we would take the time to travel to without an excuse.

We made a single pass around the shore of the lake with our ricing sticks and obtained only a handful of rice. Other ricers had obviously been here ahead of us and there was no rice left to pick. With a sigh of relief we put down the ricing sticks and picked up our fishpoles. For us the ricing season was over, and we were glad of it for we had been working day (and nights too) for a very long time and were tired. We were also flush with money and well satisfied.

Jerry poled us out of the rice and stowed the 12-foot push pole in the bottom of the canoe. We had brought no fishing gear except our fishing rods. Mine was baited with a Johnson spoon and a white pork chunk with a little tail. On each side of the tail dangled a piece of red yarn, which gave it the impression of having three tails fluttering through the water. Most of the pond was shallow and consistently weedy, but on one side the water was deeper with a point of weeds projecting into the deeper water.

I made a cast to this point and hooked a large bass. Our philosophy with Aitkin Lake bass was to get them to the boat with all possible haste before they could dive and bury themselves in the heavy weed cover. Jerry took this philosophy to the extreme. Using a short, stiff rod with 25 pound test line, he would stand up in the boat, place one foot on the gunwale, hold the rod high over his head, and reel as fast as possible, literally skittering the bass across the top of the water. To see a five-pound bass coming across the water like a weed-draped torpedo was a sight indeed.

I used a longer, more flexible rod so I wasn't able to get a bass to the boat as fast as Jerry, but I did get this particular bass to the boat in a hurry. I was excited. Not having a stringer along, Jerry tied the bass to a piece of clothesline rope found in the bottom of the canoe. I made another cast to the same spot and hooked another bass—this one larger than the first. I got him quickly to the boat and Jerry grabbed him by the mouth and hoisted him over the side. A beauty! Six pounds or more. Jerry strung the bass on the clothes line while I made another cast to the same spot. Boom! The bait had no more than touched the water when the rod was practically jerked from my still-shaking hands. The bass—I assumed it was a bass—ran out ten feet of line before I regained control of the reel handles. I reared back on the rod and the fish came out of the water. "Dogfish," I yelled, deceived by the twisting length of the fish. "Dogfish, hell!" Jerry shouted. "That's an eight pound bass!" I had the fish out in deeper water by this time and heading for the boat. "Damn," I cried, "No landing net." By this time Jerry had ripped loose the canoe's wood and rawhide seat, the rawhide sagging in the middle to form a sort of cradle. He lowered the cradle into the water. "Run him up on this," he said. When the bass was close enough, Jerry scooped him into the canoe in one swift motion, as though he had been landing bass with a boatseat all his life. Interestingly enough, they now use a similar device for landing large muskies intended for release.

Three casts. Three bass. I was still shaking and probably as excited as I have ever been. I pleaded with Jerry not to put that monster on the same water-soaked and rotten-looking piece of clothesline with the two other bass, but he simply laughed and told me not to worry.

We continued to fish this point for another half-hour and I never saw bass action comparable to this. The bass had simply gone crazy. We caught bass of every shape and description, one hardly more than three inches long. They were on one of their rare feeding sprees and who can explain why? It was perhaps ten in the morning on a bright, sunny day. Equally strange, I never caught a bass in this particular pond since, though I fished it many times thereafter.

Why did the bass decide to bite on this particular day? Had the rice harvesters, by poling through the rice in a repeated, systematic way, driven the bass out of the rice into deeper water where they were finally vulnerable to being caught? I have heard since that decaying rice gives off carbon dioxide or some other toxic gas which forces the bass to leave the ricebeds in the fall. Perhaps it was some combination of the two.

That morning, excited and happy, we made the two or three mile paddle back to the our resort and beached the canoe next to the dock. Some of my relatives were staying at the resort that Labor Day week-end and I waved them over. Soon there was a crowd gathered around our canoe, all buzzing with surprise and amazement. None of these people had ever seen bass like these.

The largest of the three bass weighed in on the resort scale at seven pounds. It won the St Paul Pioneer Press fishing contest for that week and was one of the largest bass caught in the state that summer. But Jerry and I were confident that there were even larger bass waiting to be caught in Aitkin Lake.

Catching this Labor Day bass was one of those peak experiences that remain with you always. There seemed to be many such experiences in those days, which is not too surprising. I was experiencing many of life's defining events for the first time—marriage, my first child—and each day—at least in memory—seemed fresh and exciting.

Then one day I received an alarming phone call. Jerry had suffered a serious seizure of the Grand Mal type and had been taken to the emergency room at the Veterans hospital. When he recovered, the doctors put him on anti-convulsant medication and began a long series of tests which ultimately revealed a brain tumor. The doctors operated. The tumor was malignant and so infiltrated in brain tissue that it could not be completely removed. They took what they could, and attempted to deal with the remainder with Cobalt treatments. This marked the end of Jerry as I originally knew him. There was fear in his eyes now. His zest for life largely disappeared, perhaps the result of the anti-convulsant and cobalt treatment which made him lethargic, caused a puffy weight gain, and left his curly hair falling out in patches. We still visited each other's homes and went fishing on occasion. He still played his songs of nostalgia on the piano and I recalled those times years before when the first sadness and chill began to creep into my heart.

Jerry was only in his mid-forties. He had a wife, three young children, a job that he enjoyed, and was living happily ever after in his old family home. He had everything to live for but must have sensed that he had been robbed of his future. Sadness lay heavy upon him, though he spoke lightly of his illness, was optimistic about the doctors effecting a cure, and tried hard to be cheerful.

Jerry had a grace period of perhaps two years after his initial surgery. But once the malignancy growing in his brain reached a critical mass the end came quickly. I visited him for the last time in Veterans Hospital in perhaps the same suite where I had said goodbye to Old Jim a few years before.

What shocked me most during this last visit was the look in his eyes. They were the eyes of a stranger. It was obvious to me that my friend had disappeared, and that the stranger sitting across from me could no longer be reached. Those stranger's eyes, more than anything else, broke my heart. It was a barrier I could not cross, even to say goodbye.

I have reflected many times on Jerry's life—from the time I first met him with all his wild and irrepressible vigor until he lay dying in the hospital. Little more than a dozen years had passed, yet he had gone from youth to old age to eternity like a film on fast forward. Those dozen years had wrought both fulfillment and tragedy in Jerry's short life, and I wonder if the tragedy could not have somehow been prevented. Would he have become ill if he had not taken a job which exposed him to so many dangerous chemicals? Perhaps marriage and a steady job were not the life for him. The old routine—going off every day to the same boring job—had this started to sap his energies even before he became ill?, Was he—like some wild bird—unable to prosper in captivity? This seems absurd, for Jerry was a loving and devoted father and husband. Still, I am anxious to ask him that question when we meet again on the shore of that unnamed lake where I saw him in my dream with Old Jim.

9

CONFESSIONS OF A CONFIRMED RICE BEATER

My career as a picker of wild rice began when I was 18 or 19 years old. I would have started earlier but my father was adamantly opposed to the harvest of rice by white men, believing that the rice harvest should be left to the Indians or to destitute whites who had no other means of earning money. He was no doubt right about this, but I considered myself destitute also and believed that I too had the right to earn some extra money. My decision to harvest wild rice caused some hard feelings between me and my father but since I was no longer a member of his household he could not prevent it, though I felt keenly the weight of his disapproval.

Though father might have been right, there was simply too much money to be made in wild rice for the politicians to leave it to the Indians. (They did, of course, have lakes on their reservations where only they could rice.) But to keep whites from ricing on public waters was no more feasible than decreeing that all gold in Yukon streams should belong to the natives. Perhaps it should, but try to enforce such laws when money is involved.

As it was, the Indian seldom bothered to harvest wild rice on public waters after opening day of the ricing season. After that first day the rice beds were so tangled, twisted, and destroyed that the Indians were no doubt horrified by the waste involved. To the Indian, wild rice was a source of food. To the white harvesters, it was simply a way to make money. The rice buyers paid the same price for good rice or bad. There was thus no incentive for the white harvester to wait for the rice to ripen so as to maximize the harvest. The goal was simply to beat the other fellow to it, and get as much as possible for yourself. Since you did not get involved in the processing or eating of the processed rice, you had no concern about the quality of the rice you picked. Weeds, worms and empty rice heads fetched the same price as the real thing.

The unique feature of wild rice is that the rice kernels, even on the same stalk, do not ripen together and all at once. The Indians learned to live with this characteristic. Before white men came on the scene, Indian women would go into the rice beds in their canoes and tie a number of rice plants together, much like standing shocks of corn. Tying the stalks together helped prevent ripening rice from falling into the water, and also made it easier to harvest. When the rice started to ripen, the women would paddle through the rice beds, bend the shock of rice over the side of their canoe, and gently knock loose those kernels that were ripe. They repeated this process every few days while the rice ripened.

While the modern Indian no longer bundled the rice stalks together, they still followed the practice of gradual harvest. Indians paddled their canoes through the rice beds gently, tapping the rice heads as lightly as any maestro directing a Brahms lullaby. The white man, on the other hand, wielded his ricing sticks like two clubs, beating the rice to death like a terrified person killing snakes. After a flotilla of white man's boats passed through a virgin rice bed the rice stalks were left lying in every conceivable direction, the rice twisted and snarled as though a tornado had passed through. Broken stalks, ripe rice, and entire green heads still in milk passed into the white man's boat under this brutal onslaught.

The Indians, of course, were horrified at this practice. Whereas the Indian could harvest the same rice bed for two weeks running, each day acquiring a quantity of perfectly ripe, high quality rice, the white man would destroy 90% of the rice bed in a single day.

Nobody alive and ricing at the time was a more efficient "rice clubber" than myself and my ricing partners, Jerry or Eddie. There was always a lively competition between ricers to see who could pick the most rice in a day and my partner and I were the champions in our neck of the woods. We were the best and proud of it.

Being a champion rice picker required a blend of strength, skill, endurance and intelligence. We could work all day like absolute maniacs without slackening pace or stopping except for a five-minute lunch break. But strength and endurance were not everything. The person poling the canoe had to be able to look across the field of rice—particularly after the first day—and keep the canoe in areas of good rice. After the first day, unpicked patches of virgin rice still remained but they were scarce and often difficult to get to—on a floating bog perhaps, or up near shore in water too shallow to float a canoe. In such places it took great strength and persistence on the part of the poler to put the boat in position for the "picker" (the person with the sticks) to reach the rice. The poler also needed to maintain the proper pace, pushing the canoe no faster or slower than the man with the sticks could pick the rice on both sides of the boat.

Skill was also required on the part of the picker whose only tools were the wooden ricing sticks. These sticks were fashioned from light wood—often basswood or birch—and were tapered to a point on the end, similar in looks and length to those used by a drummer in a band. A champion rice picker could play a staccato with those sticks as expertly as any drummer ever born.

The rhythm was like this: With the canoe moving continuously forward, the "picker"—who assumed a sitting or kneeling position—was required to pick the rice on both sides of the boat. Alternately, depending on which side of the boat you were picking, one stick was used to draw an armful of rice over the side of the boat, and the other stick was used to knock the kernels of rice into the boat. This was more difficult than it sounds. It was not sufficient to simply pound on the clump of rice overhanging the side of the boat. The heads of rice had to be hit just right, at a downward angle as the heads of rice pointed towards the bottom of the canoe. This type of downward strike would cause most of the rice to fall into the boat. And this was critical—getting the rice to fall into the boat. A certain amount of rice flew off into the water regardless, which was good because it helped reseed the rice bed for the following year. But your goal was not to reseed the lake but to fill your sack.

Depending upon the thickness of the bundle of rice stalks overhanging the side of the canoe, sometimes you had to hit the rice heads several times to get all the ripe rice to fall off. The general rule was that you kept hitting it until the rice kernels stopped falling. But here again skill was required. Your objective was not to simply beat the dickens out of a bundle of rice stalks, but to get the moving rice to flatten out in a thin layer across the top of your reaching stick and—at the precise moment—knock the rice off the heads with the opposite stick. Since you were picking on both sides of the boat, and the boat was moving—probably faster than you liked—it took a frantic effort to keep up. For this reason, the picker and the poler usually changed places every hour or so to give each other a break.

Another factor complicating the rice picker's task was that the rice plants did not grow to a uniform height above the water. Some rice—particularly that growing in deep water—barely projected above the sides of the canoe. Other rice, growing closer to shore—might be six feet tall. Obviously, if you bend six-foot rice stalks over the side of the canoe, it goes completely over and off the other side. The strategy here was to reach behind you as far as possible, gather in an armful of tall rice, and then—with the boat moving—wait for the heads of the tall rice to slide across your lap, at which point you struck hard with your little stick. This tall rice was usually very dense and loaded with rice kernels so it was very critical to do it right. An experienced ricer could outpick an inexperienced ricer by 10 to 1, something I saw demonstrated many times.

To us rice harvesters in the 1950's, rice was the bonanza gold, and as exciting to me as any gold rush. On opening day of the ricing season the ricing boats would be sitting cheek to jowl in the rice beds waiting for that magic hour—perhaps 9:00 AM—when the season would officially begin. At the appointed time, the poler in the rear of the boat would brandish his or her 12-foot pole with a metal duckbill on the end which prevented the pole from sinking in the mud bottom, plant the pole on the bottom of the lake and begin to push the boat forward through the rice. Most money was made that first day in virgin, unpicked rice. There was therefore a mad rush to find the thickest rice and beat the other fellow to it. That first day—in ripe rice—an experienced ricer could pick 200 or even 300 pounds of rice, which could be sold on shore that afternoon for up to a dollar a pound. After that first day, the take would drop dramatically, perhaps to 100 pounds a day if the ricing crew was ambitious and experienced. Even this reduced amount paid a far higher wage than any other work available at the time and your earnings were tax free and usually paid in cash on the spot at the end of each day. This was instant feedback as to how well you had done and how your day's work stacked up against your fellow ricers.

There was tremendous satisfaction in knowing you had done well and that there was a ready market for your work. The rice buyers waited at the boatlanding with fistfuls of cash as determined and patient as crows waiting on a road kill. Then off you would head, tired but exhilarated, to the local nightclub with a wallet full of cash and your mouth watering in anticipation of a good steak dinner.

Making good money ricing was never a sure thing. The crop could be destroyed by floods, insects, or windstorms before the season ever began. I was fortunate, during the several years that I riced, to encounter bumper rice crops almost every year.

But one had to do more than just show up with a canoe on opening day. Much of our success was due to scouting the country for unregulated rice beds which we could legally rice prior to opening day on the large lakes.

The large rice beds on such lakes as Big Sandy and Lake Minnewawa were opened by committee when the rice was deemed to be ripe. However, the general ricing season usually opened a week or so earlier, and one could legally harvest rice on small, unregulated lakes if one could find them. Some of these were no more than beaver dams or potholes in the forest which we scouted out before season and kept their existence secret. By ricing these smaller lakes, one could acquire several hundred pounds of rice before the larger lakes officially opened.

Being young, strong, and ambitious, my ricing partner and I—either Eddie or Jerry—soon discovered the location of these secret lakes near Big Sandy. One such lake lay in wild country along a roadless section of the Mississippi River. We would tow our ricing boat downriver by motorboat, and then portage our ricing boat along a dry streambed which connected the river to the lake during high water. This lake was our particular secret, and nobody ever riced it except ourselves. The rice in the lake grew sparsely, and we could pick it all in a single day, but this and other lakes like it kept us busy for that week before the "main event."

There was another much larger lake north of Big Sandy which was a solid field of rice the first time we saw it from high on a hill after a long tramp through a roadless forest. The excitement we felt upon seeing this golden bonanza lying before us can hardly be described. It was the equivalent of discovering the Mother Lode, and we could not wait to beat down the gates and sack this golden city before us.

Unfortunately there was no easy way in, or at least none that was open to us. Someone owned land to the south, and there was a locked gate guarding the single logging road leading towards the lake. Eddie and I had to gain our access from the north, a mile down a muddy logging road where my low-slung 41 Cadillac repeatedly got mired in mud. Then there was a half-mile carry through trackless and nearly impenetrable forest with our heavy wooden ricing boat and all our gear. The boat, even before it became waterlogged and even heavier, must have weighed 150 pounds, and there was no good way to carry it except on your shoulders. So the two of us stumbled through the forest, the boat bruising our shoulders, the hazel brush slapping us in the face with every step, tangled roots and deadfalls occasionally tripping us up. Then the heavy boat would come crashing down upon us like some falling tree.

We reached the lake with our boat finally, and made a return trip to the car for our push pole, ricing sticks, and gunny sacks for bagging the rice. We pushed out into this golden field of grain, our hearts beating with anticipation. But alas! The rice was still quite green. For the next three or four days we clubbed ourselves and the reluctant rice heads into a state of exhaustion for 10 hours a day and acquired perhaps 100 pounds a day of green, poor quality rice. This was not quite the bonanza we had been anticipating, but it was adequate to hold our interest. But it was long, boring, and backbreaking work. One cold day we both fell out of the boat and worked wet the rest of the day, close to hypothermia, though at the time we had never heard the word. Then, after 10 hours of ricing, there was the long carry of your heavy rice sacks through the forest, a muddy logging road to traverse, and a late supper which you were almost too tired to eat.

But this muddy logging road sticks in my mind as one of the defining events of my life. Heading out of this logging road one afternoon, we bumped into my ricing partner's brother Bob, who later served many years as Minnesota District Court Judge, with chambers in Aitkin. Bob had been after me to go on to college, and this day he carried with him an application to the University of Minnesota, Duluth, which he had picked up earlier and had been meaning to give me. That application, obtained so unexpectedly in such an unlikely spot, certainly changed the direction of my life. I had always wanted to attend college, but had procrastinated for several years and undoubtedly—without that application in my hand—would have continued to procrastinate. But now Bob had me on the spot and feeling obligated. If he could take the trouble to bring me an application, the least I could do was to fill it out and send it in. So I did, but that is the subject of another chapter.

As I became more experienced in the ricing business, my partner and I looked for ways to increase our income. Being good entrepreneurs, we decided to add a second shift to our operation—to rice illegally at night. Now it made no sense to rice at night once the season was open and the rice picked over. No, if one were to make money ricing at night it had to be done in ripe, unpicked rice before season. What made this feasible was the way the rice season was controlled on the larger lakes. A committee of local experts—some Indians among them—monitored the rice beds and decided when the rice was ripe enough to harvest. This committee, who could not monitor all the lakes within their jurisdiction, seldom opened the season on a date which pleased everyone. Perhaps this was impossible due to the differing ripening dates on different lakes. At any rate, when the season was finally opened, the rice would be green on one lake and dead ripe and falling in the water in another. It was on one of these lakes where the rice was dead ripe that we decided to make our first stab at night ricing.

One moonlight night in late August Eddie and I paddled our rice boat across the bay from our resort and began ricing in a secluded backwater behind the island where old John Nelson had once lived alone in his tiny cabin. It was a beautiful warm night, without insects to bother us, and the rising moon flooded the rice fields with a golden, peaceful glow. Eddie and I spoke in whispers, not because we were afraid of being overheard, but because there was an awesome hush in the air that we were loath to disturb. The only sound was an occasional splash of the rice pole and the "whish, whish" of the rice sticks as I struck the rice.

Suddenly we heard a crashing in the dark woods bordering our bay. We stopped to listen, our hearts in our throats. An instant later a voice rang out from somewhere in the shadows close to shore: "Hey, you guys. Come over here!" The game warden! We were caught redhanded! We would lose our boat, our license, the privilege of ricing this season. "What should we do?" Eddie asked. "Head for shore," I whispered. The voices continued to shout at us to stop.

When our boat touched shore, Eddie and I leaped out, hoisted the heavy boat—now half full of rice—unto our shoulders, and ran with it through the woods. Our goal was to cross the island, launch our boat on the opposite side, and take off paddling for parts unknown.

But too late! We could hear our pursuers panting through the darkened woods behind, shouting occasionally for us to stop. I told Eddie to drop the boat and swim for it. It would have been a long swim in any direction.

I was in water up to my waist when I heard someone talking. They had caught Eddie. Then I heard someone laugh and call me by name. It was a voice I recognized—one of my high school friends. I sighed in relief and heaved myself out of the cold water. There was a lot of nervous laughing and joking as we gathered around our boat and compared stories. They had arrived in the same bay ahead of us and were fortunate enough to hear us coming, giving them a chance to hide. When they realized we were simply other poachers, they decided to make their presence known. They really had no choice for we had them pinned down on shore. We could hardly believe the coincidence of the two of us picking the same bay to rice in this labyrinth of bays and islands.

The four of us picked up our heavy rice boat, still half full of rice, and began staggering with it through the darkness back the way we had come. Every 100 feet or so we had to put down the boat and rest. It's indicative of our terror that Eddie and I were able to run through a dark woods with the heavy boat on our shoulders for over a quarter mile without stopping. Now four of us—all big, strong men—could hardly pick it up.

Eventually we arrived back at our original destination and proceeded to harvest wild rice for what remained of the night. But this experience so traumatized Eddie and I that we gave up ricing at night for a long time.

The risk was too great, we decided. It was quite clear to both of us that if we could bump into friends in a nameless bay in the dead of night we could meet the game warden there also.

Three or four years were to pass before I tried night ricing again. My partner Eddie had gone off to the Air Force and I was now ricing with Jerry who was older than I and more willing to take a risk. Also, the price of green rice had continued to rise and the potential rewards were greater.

Jerry and I planned our strategy carefully. The finest rice in Aitkin County and perhaps the entire state came from Lake Minnewawa which lay just to the south of Big Sandy. For some strange reason—whether better genetics or water chemistry—the kernels of Lake Minnewawa rice were nearly an inch long and delectable to eat. It also fetched a price 15 to 20 percent higher than ordinary rice. If we were going to take the risk of ricing at night, why not go after the best?

But how to get access to this rice? The rice grew in the middle of a bay in full view of dozens of summer and year-around cottages. All of these were built along a road which paralleled the north side of the lake. We would certainly be seen or heard if we attempted to gain access off this road. Indeed, we would be forced to walk though somebody's yard to get to the lake.

My wife Kathy had the answer. Her father had logged on the south side of the lake a few years earlier and had pushed a logging road to within a quarter mile of the water's edge just south of the Lake Minnewawa rice beds. Kathy and her father had often used this logging road as a launching point for hunting ducks on Lake Minnewawa. This old and long-abandoned logging road was perfect for our purpose—totally isolated and known to only a few. Nor were there any farms or cabins nearby to see us entering or leaving the woods.

We reconnoitered the lake one evening just as the sun was setting. It looked perfect, the rice beds no more than a quarter-mile offshore and aglow with a golden light from the late afternoon sun. There were no cabins at all on this side of the lake and we could paddle to the rice beds unobserved by anyone.

A day or two later we drove to the end of the road just as it was getting dark and carried our canoe down an overgrown trail to the shore of the lake where he hid our canoe where it could not be seen from either the trail or the lake. By now it was totally dark and we managed to get lost while returning to my car which I had left with the engine running. For the next hour we wandered about in the dark and brushy woods before stumbling out onto the logging road just as the car's engine was bucking, wheezing, and about to boil over from overheating.

The next evening we launched our canoe in darkness and crossed the quarter-mile of open water to the ricebed, which we had not yet seen up close. We each eagerly grabbed a handful of riceheads to check for ripeness. The rice was dead ripe and came off in our hands to the gentlest touch. If we had dared shout we would have done so such was our excitement and elation. The size of the rice kernels shocked us. Never had we seen such wonderful rice and now we had it all to ourselves. We riced all that night and came off the lake just before dawn with 200 pounds of choice rice in the bottom of our canoe.

The next night we gave Lake Minnewawa a rest and riced instead on Aitkin Lake. Our great fear was that our nocturnal activities would be detected by warden patrol planes which might overfly the ricebeds during the day. This was not an idle fear for a ricing boat left trails through the ricebeds much like a wandering moose would leave in a ripe field of wheat. The heavier and thicker the rice, the more obvious the trail. On Lake Minnewawa the rice grew in six feet of water and was of only medium height. We were hopeful that this type of rice would spring back after our canoe passed through, thus concealing our trails. We were also banking heavily on our secret escape route through the woods on the south side of the bay. If a game warden approached our ricebed at night—either by motor or paddling, we thought we would hear him in time to slip away in the darkness. This of course was foolish thinking indeed. A fast boat with a searchlight would have caught us in a hurry. And today, with night vision binoculars, the game warden could have watched our every move without leaving shore.

But we were wise to vary the location of our nocturnal and highly illegal activates. We learned later that the game warden had spent many sleepless nights that week staking out a watch on one lake after another. We were lucky enough to stay one jump ahead of him, to zig when he zagged, so to speak. But this was due to luck rather than any brilliance on our part. And we were probably aided by the activities of other poachers. It is quite possible that every lake in the country was being riced illegally that week and the game warden had been chasing others as well as ourselves.

At any rate, we were not caught or even pursued, but the suspense and tension we were under is difficult to imagine. It was one of the most exciting weeks of my life. At night, one quickly begins to hallucinate, particularly when under stress and staring into the darkness. Those cabin lights on shore, are they moving? Is it a flashlight coming in our direction? A bobbing light on the bow of a boat? What was that noise? Sound travels an infinite distance across water and particularly at night. We heard every sound. The land itself seemed to be breathing, skulking in the shadows, dangerous. Why had that dog suddenly began to bark? Had it detected our presence somehow and was giving the alarm? Was the dog's owner even now phoning the game warden who lived next door to Lake Minnewawa? How long would it take him to arrive?

By dawn every nerve was on edge, our senses overwrought from staring into the darkness and seeing danger, movement, flashing lights everywhere we looked. We were surrounded by alien noises, some which we made ourselves and wished we could prevent. The dip of the pushpole in the water sounded as loud as the splashings of a whale. The slap of the ricing sticks against the rice seemed as noisy as a drum roll in a marine band.

One night as we riced we watched a thunderstorm building in the northwest. At first it was simply dull flashes of light and muffled booms as though from artillery fire on a far-off battlefield. Then the churning storm front moved closer, its darker blackness clearly delineated against the star-studded sky as though troweled on by a careless artist. Jagged lightning strikes sawed through the rolling clouds followed by a tremendous clap of thunder.

The rice was falling into our canoe wonderfully well and neither Jerry or I wanted to quit. The boat was three-quarters full of golden rice and we wanted more. We continued to rice while anxiously watching the storm front move closer. Now the lightning strike and the thunderclap were almost simultaneous. Time to go! We stowed the rice pole and paddled frantically for shore, the canoe full of rice to the gunnel and difficult to move. A blast of wind shot out of the night unexpectedly, fortunately on our backs and helping to drive us forward. We hit shore with a jump, bagged our rice, hid the canoe, and ran with the heavy bags up the wooded ridge towards our car. There was no rain as yet but the wind was howling overhead and the sky was bright as day with continuous lightning strikes.

We drove home and had no more than entered Old Jim's porch when a large oak fell on a neighboring cabin and the electricity went off. A deafening roar passed overhead, either from a tornado or a hurricane-force wind.

We poured ourselves coffee from our nearly empty thermos, lit a cigarette, and sat there in the darkness about as happy as we had ever been in our lives. Our adrenalin and prayers of thanksgiving were both flowing freely. There was tremendous satisfaction in knowing that we had safely got off the lake with our rice before the tornado struck. If we had been caught on the water in our overloaded canoe…well, we could imagine the consequences.

And at the time we did not know the worst of it. We found out later that our wood and canvas canoe, which we had recently given a coat of fiberglass to prevent it from leaking, no longer floated when capsized.

We discovered this dangerous flaw a week later when the boat took on water near shore on Aitkin Lake and sank like a stone with the two of us in it, Jerry still standing up to his chest in water in the rear of the submerged canoe trying to push it to shore.

"Stop pushing, you damn fool," I said with a laugh. "This boat wasn't made to travel on the bottom."

The night of the storm was our last night of ricing on Lake Minnewawa. The official season was to open in a day or two and we thought we had pushed our luck far enough. We already had a 1000 pounds of rice stashed in Old Jim's garage and were well pleased with ourselves, particularly our success in avoiding detection.

But we had not fooled our observant neighbor next door, the mother of my previous ricing partner, Eddie. For several days running she had noticed, each morning, wet ricing clothes hanging on the outdoor clothes line. And she noticed also how—each evening—these same clothes would disappear from the line just before dark. This phenomenon of the appearing and disappearing clothes might have puzzled her momentarily, but not for long. One day that week she gave me a good scolding about it (I was like one of her sons), but I neither admitted or denied anything.

On the day the official ricing season opened on Big Sandy and Lake Minnewawa Jerry and I sold over a thousand pounds of rice to our local ricebuyer as premium Lake Minnewawa rice. The rice buyer must have wondered how anyone could harvest a half-ton of rice on Lake Minnewawa in a single day, but he asked no questions. Perhaps he should have, because only half the rice we sold that day actually came from Lake Minnewawa. To our shame (though we thought it clever at the time), we had put ordinary rice on the bottom of our sacks with the Lake Minnewawa rice on top to a sufficient depth that the rice buyer would reach only Minnewawa rice when he plunged his arm into the sack to check for quality.

Rice buyers were a shrewd lot, difficult to fool, and after gaining experience we quit trying to fool them (with the exception I just mentioned). When we first started ricing we would bag up everything in the bottom of the boat: heads off the rice, cattail stalks, aquatic weeds dredged up from the depths by our ricing pole—you name it. But the rice buyer would invariably dig through the sack—as far as arm could reach—and bring forth these hidden treasures, fixing us as he did so with a mournful, pitying look while we were subjected to the scornful guffaws of other ricers who happened to be standing around watching. After this happened once or twice we decided honesty was the best policy, and I went to the opposite extreme, meticulously picking out every broken leaf and weed before bagging the rice. Thereafter, the rice we sold was about as perfectly clean as one could find.

Our reputation for selling clean rice no doubt was what allowed us to fool the ricebuyer on a grand scale when we topped off our bags of low grade rice with Lake Minnewawa rice. Whether this trick was discovered we never knew. The buyer never mentioned it and remained our friend. No doubt he was paid a premium for buying Lake Minnewawa rice just as we were paid a premium for selling it.

There was only once—a few years earlier—when we again engaged in outright fraud, and that was because we believed that the rice buyer—a different buyer who was not our friend—was attempting to cheat us. This unhappy (but highly satisfying) event occurred late in the season one year when the rice crop had been nearly devoured by worms.

I have not mentioned the worms thus far in this narrative but they deserve mention because they contributed mightily to making the picking of wild rice not a job for the squeamish. The worms were perhaps a half-inch long and looked like tiny caterpillars, which in fact is what they were. The worms hatched from eggs deposited on the rice plant by tiny moths, and they spent a part of their life cycle feeding on the ripe kernels of rice.

Unavoidably, when you knocked rice kernels into the boat you knocked the worms in also, and in years of high worm infestation they were nearly as plentiful as the rice. There were millions of the nasty creatures and at times the piled up rice in the bottom of the canoe was literally moving as the tiny creatures broke surface and inched their way across the top of the rice. Being present in almost infinite numbers, it was only a matter of time until they inched their way up the leg of your trousers and settled in every fleshy crevice they found, particularly around the midriff, where most of us have a roll or two when sitting. Any worm penetrating one of these fleshy crevices would inevitably be pinched as you leaned forward to reach for an armful of rice. A pinced worm is a biting worm and the little devils could bite something fierce. One learned to tolerate the bites as an occupational hazard, and we also learned to keep our shirt tucked in and our belt tight to prevent the worm from gaining access.

However, we did not really begrudge the presence of the worms for they added weight to the bag of rice and fetched the same price as the rice itself. Unfortunately, they would not stay in the bag but crawled out through holes in the burlap to infest your car if you were unfortunate enough to have to put the bags in the car's trunk. One found worms crawling about the car seats for weeks afterward, and only a good freeze would put an end to their meanderings.

The fraud incident I mentioned earlier took place during a year of particularly heavy worm infestation. They had devoured the rice crop so thoroughly that most of the rice kernels were simply empty chaff. One could tell the quality of the rice to a certain extent by hefting and noting how heavy it was. This particular year the bags of rice were light as a feather.

We had sold all our rice this year to the same rice buyer. This particular day he offered 20 cents a pound less than he had been paying us, and this was not the first time he had dropped his price. No doubt he had good reason to do so.

But Eddie and I were highly offended and refused to sell to him, taking the rice instead to another buyer. This buyer refused to take it at any price. However, he gave us some sound advice and made us a promise. If we would take the rice home and separate the good rice from the chaff, he would pay us triple the going price. This was easier than it might sound, for if you put rice in a large tub of water, the chaff will float while the sound kernels sink to the bottom.

This separation was also more difficult than it sounds, for you could only process a few handfuls at a time and we worked at it till late in the night. Eventually the job was complete, and we put the result of our long effort into two bags—one containing the good rice and the other containing the chaff. The good rice we sold to the buyer who had suggested the sorting process for $1.20 a pound. The chaff we sold to the first buyer at his original offer of 55 cents a pound. The net effect of all this (besides a guilty conscience) was that we were paid $1.75 a pound for the worst rice we had ever picked.

Not wishing to press our luck by trying this ruse again, we hung up our ricing sticks for the season. As always, the rice harvest had been a great adventure as well as profitable. I had just received word that my application to UMD had been accepted, and I was to appear on campus the coming Saturday to write an essay which would determine whether I needed some remedial English classes before I could enroll in Freshman English.

I made a trip to Brainerd where I had been working that summer for the DNR and spent $600 of my ricing money on a new wardrobe which I thought would be appropriate for a young blade about to enter college. I was 21, owned a reliable car (a 52 Chrysler New Yorker), had money in the bank, no responsibilities, and a new world waiting to be conquered.

10

THE LINCOLN AND THE CADILLAC

In the summer of 1952 an overloaded '51 Buick station wagon with drying diapers pinched tight in its rolled-up windows pulled into the driveway of our store on the highway and life in the little town of Libby was never afterwards the same.

The diapers, now that the car had stopped, no longer flopped in the breeze, but settled down over the windows like curtains so that one could not see in. But then the doors were flung open and out piled eight or ten children of every conceivable size and age. There were toddlers among them, girls of high school age, and undoubtedly babes in arms if the diapers were any indication. For a moment they stood there beside the car blinking and stretching, and then began nosing about like a bunch of pups suddenly turned loose in a new place. This was my first introduction to the Sylvester Graff family, who would be my neighbors, companions, and good friends for the rest of my life.

Living as we did in a neighborhood so small that one could throw a stone from one end to the other, the arrival of strangers was always a cause for excitement. I noticed that there were pretty girls in the car and handsome young men, enough to give my sister and I some competition in our daily touch football games in front of our old store on the lake. Here were possibilities unlimited—future girlfriends, hunting companions, friends to entertain us on the interminable ride on the school bus to McGregor. This 36-mile ride twice a day, which took us nearly to Palisade, came close to destroying the sanity of both the children and the bus driver. Some new companions would certainly make the ride more interesting.

We discovered shortly that the family was looking to purchase a retirement home on the lake, and they soon found one—a large house only two doors to the south of our resort. These people were to be our neighbors, which might prove interesting, yet they were strangers, and might prove dangerous. My sister Ann and I had met enough strange children at the resort that we knew enough to be cautious until we had a chance to see what these new people were like. As the new kids on the block, it was up to them, or so we thought, to demonstrate why we should like them. But one cannot remain aloof for long with people who are practically your only neighbors—particularly not this crew who proved to be friendly, outgoing and persistently talkative. The boys in particular had a million questions about their new surroundings and asked them incessantly with a funny drawl which seemed to me to be out of the deep south, but which proved to be no more than a Midwestern twang from the state of Kansas. The boys, as young as they were, were wildly enthusiastic about hunting and fishing, an enthusiasm I shared. We quickly became friends.

So the family settled in next door and doubled the population of Libby in a single stroke. The patriarch of the family—old Sylvester—was a handsome, still vigorous man in his forties who wore pork chop sideburns, chewed snoose, and walked with a slight stoop as though bearing a heavy load. With a dozen children to raise, he was indeed under a heavy load, though he never gave indication that this load was unwelcome, or bothersome. On the contrary, his children—particularly the girls—appeared to give him the greatest pleasure and with them he had the patience of Job.

Perhaps a heavier responsibility was his decision to retire at age forty with eight dependent children still living under his roof. However, he gave no indication of worrying about that either. Perhaps he left all the worrying to his wonderful wife, Mae.

The mother of the clan (Mother Mae) was several years younger than Sylvester, a strong, still-attractive lady who ruled over her family—particularly the girls in the family—with an iron fist. To the daughters she provided stern and loving discipline, religious instruction, and sage advice, though she had a tendency to spoil her three sons, waiting on them hand and foot as though they and their father were some kind of royalty. The boys thus grew up to expect women to wait on them and they were lucky enough (or astute enough) to marry strong and good women who would.

But Mother Mae was consistent in this. She catered to Sylvester in the same way, fetching his slippers or a favorite pipe, slipping a footstool under his weary feet on a cold winter evening. In truth, Mother Mae treated Sylvester like a king, and these acts—as I interpreted them—were not performed from a sense of duty but from an enduring love that never varied as long as they lived. Even in their sixties and seventies Mother Mae could be found sitting on Sylvester's lap in the evening, the two of them cuddling like the most ardent lovebirds.

When the Graff family arrived at Sandy Lake in the early 1950's there were eight children still living at home. Their ages ranged from 16 down to 2 or 3. Despite this brood of dependent children, Sylvester had decided to retire and was now putting wish into action. Any financial planner would have considered such a plan insane, and so it was. A man in his forties with eight growing and perpetually hungry children is fortunate not to starve, much less retire. But apparently Sylvester saw no obstacles to this plan. Somehow he had managed to save enough money—perhaps two or three thousand dollars—to pay cash for this large old house on the lake which sat on perhaps 10 acres of hill. The house had electricity but no plumbing except for a hand pump in the kitchen. The bathroom was a two-hole outhouse some 75 feet from the house which must have been a busy place both winter and summer considering the depth of the dirt path leading in its direction.

There was no central heating. Any heat that managed to make it to the upper level of this two-story home came either from a fieldstone fireplace or a potbelly woodstove which sat in a corner of the dining room. Fortunately, there were no water pipes to freeze, but the family must have done some shivering in their upstairs bedrooms.

But considering the time and place, this was a very nice house on a choice piece of lakeshore and Sylvester had selected well. The home's previous owner had established a large garden on a level area behind the house. He had also planted crabapple trees on a sunny slope behind the garden, and these trees had been bearing apples for many years. The lake, just off shore of Sylvester's dock, was full of fish which were usually biting. Across the bay the great wildrice beds began which extended all the way to Aitkin Lake. All in all, if it were possible to feed oneself and live off the land anywhere this might be the place. And the experiment was not without precedent. In this very place the Sioux, the Ojibwae, and other earlier Indian tribes had lived off the land for centuries.

Living off the land—no matter how fruitful that land might be—still requires a certain amount of cash money to buy incidentals and pay taxes. Sylvester had this need covered. At some point in his earlier life he had purchased or built a small apartment building in Kansas which paid him a small monthly income. This income was perhaps no more than a pittance, but it was apparently enough.

I go into detail on the family finances only because it has a bearing on the story that follows. Anyone can retire if they have enough money. But to retire without money requires both courage and creativity. Sylvester was about to embark on a attempt to live the good life without working and without money, and to raise a large family of dependents besides. What made this experiment in living interesting to me is that it was totally opposed to my own family's way of life and contrary to everything my own father believed.

To retire at forty with a growing family was, in my father's eyes, both crazy and irresponsible. For an able-bodied man not to work was sinful and perhaps even a bit subversive. It just wasn't done. There were others in the country who did not work but they were either half-crazy old hermits who lived alone or old retirees who had earned the right to spend their few remaining days at leisure. Sylvester fit neither of these profiles. Here was a strong man in the prime of life about to go on perpetual vacation. Father was shocked by the idea and could hardly restrain his disapproval. What would happen to this family? What dire consequences would befall the children? Children needed discipline and to be taught to work. How could they be taught to work by a father who refused to work himself? This was certainly a tragedy in the making.

Such were perhaps my father's thoughts as Sylvester moved in next door. Both men were close to the same age. Both were strong, vigorous men of independent spirit. Both had attitudes toward work and a philosophy of life totally opposed to each other. Both came from long-lived ancestors—which would give the two men the next half century to live out their alternate lifestyles. If they could not prove their point through argument, then they would prove it in the most persuasive way possible—by living it.

None of this conflict was ever stated or even acknowledged by the two men as far as I know. Indeed, they would have scoffed that such a rivalry was occurring. And it was not occurring in any overt way. The two men simply did their own thing for the next 40 years, but they did it with each other as a witness.

Now you can not live your life in front of a witness—particularly a witness who disagrees or disapproves of the way you are living your life—without it affecting your own behavior in some fashion. As a minimum, having an audience might cause you to be a little more deliberate in your actions—perhaps even to the point of exaggerating those qualities which offend the other party.

I do not know whether father's intent was to make Sylvester feel guilty, or if Sylvester's hope was to make my father feel envy, but I am quite sure—if such were the case—that neither succeeded. For the next forty years Sylvester watched father work while father watched

Sylvester play and the disapproval both men felt must have strengthened and enriched both their lives.

Sylvester liked to sit in his boat with one of his daughters and fish all day in full view of my father who was scrubbing out 15 boats, carrying heavy outboard motors to and from the boathouse, cutting acres of grass, and a multitude of other strenuous activities. What did father think as he watched Sylvester, through a haze of sweat and weariness, sitting out there in quiet water, pulling in enough perch and rock bass to feed the family fish dinner? What did Sylvester think as he watched father perform his heavy labors, too busy to hardly stop for dinner, or to eat it without interruption? Perhaps neither man gave it a thought, and this unstated rivalry I thought I saw was simply the work of my imagination. I did know, as I watched these two pursuing their respective lifestyles, that there were no winners or losers here. Both men were doing exactly what they wanted to be doing. Father detested leisure as much as Sylvester despised repetitive, pointless work. Father's work was both his occupation and his recreation, and the same could be said for Sylvester's leisure.

"Dad is the strongest man I ever saw," remarked one of Sylvester's daughters one day in my father's presence. "He ought to be," my father grunted. "He's never used any of it."

But Sylvester was far from being a lazy man. He simply worked when he felt like working at those things that struck his fancy. As a matter of fact he was usually busy doing something—puttering about the garage, hoeing the garden, hauling firewood in the back of his ancient station wagon. And of course he spent a good deal of time fishing, though this may have been more in the nature of a necessity than total pleasure. Keeping a family warm and fed takes an enormous amount of time as anyone who has lived off the land can attest.

But father looked upon Sylvester's busyness as simply a means of avoiding "real work," which meant the kind you got paid for. The purpose of life was to produce something, to create wealth, to leave the world a little better than you found it. Sylvester was apparently producing nothing. He was simply frittering away his meager capital and when that was gone the family would starve.

From time to time Sylvester would come into our store and buy a can of Copenhagen with the exact number of coins in his hand. Apparently this was his only luxury and indulgence. Father, if he were waiting on the store that day, would take Sylvester's money and pass him the Copenhagen with hardly a word. They seldom had much to say upon meeting, their philosophies so opposed that they walked carefully, tiptoeing around each other and around issues as stiff and formal as two rival mastiffs who—whether out of mutual fear or respect—have chosen neither to fight or to become friendly. This situation prevailed for 40 years.

But despite an apparent lack of cash money, the Graff family did not appear to be suffering. They built a shed on their property from cast-off slabs of lumber from a nearby sawmill and purchased a milk cow which lived in the shed during the winter. The cow provided the family with milk, cream, and butter. They raised chickens for both meat and eggs, and lived off fresh garden produce in the summer, canning the excess for winter use.

In the fall, Sylvester and Mae harvested wild rice together for two or three weeks and made enough money to purchase a luxury or two: a new television set, an indoor toilet. The Graff sons were excellent hunters and crack shots, quite capable of keeping wild game on the table. They lived on venison, bear, squirrel, grouse, waterfowl, as well as plenty of fish—a healthy diet indeed. Every Sunday the family scrubbed up and went to church, the old Buick station wagon older now, and sagging on its springs. Sylvester kept this vehicle running for years beyond its normal lifespan. He nursed a single set of spark plugs for 100,000 miles, and was quite capable of adjusting the vehicle's points with no fancier tool than a jackknife should the car stall along the highway on the way to church. He rummaged through junkyards for used parts and old tires and kept the Buick running year after year with hardly any cash expenditure.

All of the above took time, but time was something Sylvester had in abundance. He was demonstrating an often forgotten point—that time truly is money and a substitute for it. What seemed ironic to me, is that while father labored and made money while Sylvester rested and made none, the standard of living of our two families was quite similar. Both father and Sylvester were frugal, conservative men who drove used cars and avoided ostentation. We probably ate more beef and pork, but they had more time to eat and enjoy whatever was put on the table. In the summer our family ate on the run and could seldom finish a meal without interruption. I could not help but wonder why one should become a slave to work and waiting on customers if one could live nearly as well without working. This, of course, was the exact point Henry David Thoreau made in "Walden" about the poor farmer who labored from daylight till dark simply to feed a voracious appetite caused by the nature of his backbreaking labors. If he worked less, he could survive on less food and thus have more freedom.

But this was not simply an economic issue but a moral one. Work was not only good for the soul but essential in a modern economy. What would happen to the world if everyone stopped working? We would revert to a nation of hunter/gatherers like the Sioux and Ojibwae we had supplanted. These tribes had warred for generations over scarce resources. Today, resources were even more scarce and the population had exponentially expanded. War, chaos, and starvation would result if everyone attempted to return to the land.

Of course, father was not concerned that Sylvester's lifestyle and recalcitrance would destroy the country. But he did have concern that it would encourage the Graff children to a life of laziness and irresponsibility.

Strangely enough, this did not appear to be happening—at least, not to the daughters. Most of the Graff girls worked at our resort at one time or another. They were all fine young ladies, bright and hardworking. If the Graff children were going to be ruined by their father's refusal to work, which was what father predicted, there was no sign of it here.

Father agreed that the Graff daughters seemed to be turning out just fine. In fact, he admired them very much. But the sons would not be so fortunate, One learned by example. If the father refused to work, wasting his days hunting and fishing and other frivolous pursuits, why should the sons be any different? I could not dispute father's logic because I was a product of his training and mostly agreed with it. Although I disliked much of the work I was required to do, and left home as soon as possible to avoid it, I believed—and still believe—that discipline and hard work as a youth are good for the soul. But the Graff sons did not appear to be doing too badly either. All three completed high school, went on to college, and completed advanced degrees—two of the boys in law. The eldest son, who was two years my junior, encouraged me to go on to college and was my roommate for a time. Two or three years after graduating from law school, he ran for an Aitkin county judgeship, was elected, and spent the rest of his working days as an Aitkin County judge. The youngest son practiced law for a time, worked as an IRS agent, and went on to other government positions. The middle son, Edward, my hunting companion and ricing partner, spent his working career—along with his wife—teaching Eskimos and Indians in far-off lands—until retiring in his early fifties in the old family home on Sandy Lake.

So what had occurred here? This was not the way this scenario was supposed to play out. Where were the tragic results of Sylvester's lifestyle on the upbringing of his three sons?

As the years passed, and father and Sylvester grew older, a little more warmth—or perhaps simply tolerance—seemed to creep into their relationship. By this time father must have accepted the fact that Sylvester had no intentions of either working or starving.

And then father won a victory of sorts. Father was on the McGregor School Board, and the Sandy Lake area needed a bus driver. Would Sylvester be interested in the job? To father's great amazement,

Sylvester agreed, and I believe I understand why. This job, which would require two or three hours of his time each day, was no sacrifice at all. Sylvester was finally going to be paid for something he had been doing the past 30 years for free—driving a noisy load of kids to town. What could be easier? After years of driving around his own noisy brood, he knew how to tune out chaos. For both my father and Sylvester, this job was strictly win-win. Father had finally got old Sylvester to take a paying job. And Sylvester, to his way of thinking, had still not gone to work.

The bus driving job undoubtedly added to the family's comfort in later years. With additional money to spend, Mae added a modern bathroom to the house, upgraded the kitchen, and installed central heating so they no longer had to depend on wood to heat the house. Eventually they built a comfortable apartment above their garage which was easier to heat during the winter. The large family home on the hill they sold to their son.

So the saga of the Sylvester Graff family was coming to an end. Sylvester and mother Mae were living comfortably on the shores of the lake where they had spent their last 40 years, still surrounded by children and grandchildren. They had succeeded in living the good life, and had taught their children to do the same.

Father's prognostications of disaster for this family obviously missed the mark by a wide margin. What had happened here? Here were two families growing up and growing old side by side—ourselves and the Graffs—who were living our lives according to quite different philosophies—both theoretical and in practice—yet the outcomes for us children were practically identical. It seems clear to me now in retrospect that there were some great sources of strength and lessons being taught in the Graff family that were not apparent on the surface. Of course, there was the strong religious and moral foundation established by mother Mae. The children were taught to pray, and like many practicing Catholic families, were required to pray daily. In addition to their catechism, mother Mae taught them discipline, honesty, and the value of a dollar.

Sylvester was less engaged in the training of the children, but taught by example and the example was of great value. Sylvester, after all, had worked as a young man, saved every penny, and had acquired the capital needed to retire by the time he was forty. What better example could one provide of the value of being frugal, delaying gratification, and saving your money? Only in this way could one escape the slave labor economy of hard work and low pay which entrapped so many of Sylvester's generation. Once I thought about it, I realized that father had followed the same path as Sylvester. Father had worked hard, saved his money, and then—instead of retiring like Sylvester—had purchased a resort which allowed him to spend the rest of his life doing what he loved to do. The two men were more alike than they knew. They simply called freedom by different names. And neither man was truly free. Father labored to serve the public. Sylvester labored to feed, clothe, and house his family.

Sylvester's decision to move with his family to a small plot of land in the country was the act of a rebel and also of a hero. Not only is the land against you but so are your working neighbors who often resent the attempt. Today, the desire to live a more meaningful life in the country is better understood, and is in fact the lifelong dream of hordes of harried city dwellers. But Sylvester was a pioneer. His was the philosophy that started Mother Earth News, the Foxfire Books, and made heroes of Helen and Scott Nearing, the gurus of the back-to-the-land movement.

This life is obviously not for everyone. It was not a life the Graff children wanted to live. Having lived it, they did not romanticize it. They knew very well the hard work and self denial involved. They also knew that they had not earned it yet and needed to spend their own season in the world of commerce.

Despite their limited finances, mother Mae—who was the family's banker and financial wizard—was quite willing to help the children get on in the world. One of the very interesting interactions I saw occurring in this family was their willingness to lend money to each other for worthwhile purposes such as transportation or education. What is just as surprising, they always paid each other back. There was therefore trust in the family in regard to finances. The message was clear: it was acceptable to borrow money but you had to pay it back, and promptly. I don't know what threats mother Mae used to instill this lesson (it must have been the threat of death, or something like it), but none of the children, to my knowledge, ever failed to pay back a family debt. It just was not done. And I believe that this access to money from family members during times of real need had much to do with the future career and financial success of the Graff children.

At age 67, father finally sold the resort and retired, 30 years after Sylvester's own retirement. Now, the lifestyles of the two men became nearly identical. Both men spent a good deal of time in their gardens, gathering firewood, enjoying their grandchildren, and a host of similar activities. Father had moved down the road, away from the Graff home, but the road was on a curving bay so that father could look directly across the bay and observe Sylvester's activities with even greater clarity than before. I am not stating with certainty that the two men paid any attention to what the other was doing, but it would be difficult not to.

Even in retirement, father remained busier than Sylvester. Father took up maple sugaring, and spent three weeks in the spring tapping over 100 maple trees and boiling down the gathered sap to make maple syrup. He continued his activity in Aitkin County politics, serving as a volunteer and campaign manager for several state congressmen. Father and Sylvester were both Democrats, but not surprisingly found themselves on opposite factions of the Democratic party. These two factions were as contentious with each other—perhaps more so—then they were with their Republican rivals. And father threw his support for county judge behind a man who just happened to be the bitter rival of

Sylvester's eldest son, who repeatedly won re-election despite father's support of his opponent.

As I mentioned before, father and Sylvester were near the same age. As they reached their eighties, it seemed that Sylvester's laid-back life-style had proven itself superior to the life of hard work chosen by father. Those years had taken their toll on father's body. He had severely damaged his back logging, and—though Mayo surgeons had partially repaired the damage—he was left with a stiff back which made bending difficult. Because he could not easily bend, He was forced to do much of his work—such as painting, or finishing cement slabs—on his knees. Fifty years of this activity destroyed the cartilage in his knees and made walking both difficult and painful. When the pain or lack of mobility became unendurable, he checked into the hospital and had one of his knee joints replaced with a plastic version. Both knees were wrecked and needed to be replaced. However, father balked when the doctors informed him that the plastic knee would not support as much weight as the original, and would curtail his heavy lifting. Father apparently had visions of his two plastic knees collapsing under the weight of a heavy load, so he decided to keep one of his original knees just in case. This was a decision he regretted. At age 90 he requested the operation, but the doctors declined, fearing that father could not withstand the trauma of surgery.

By this time father had been under the surgeon's knife a number of times. He had undergone spinal fusion, had his knee replaced, his gall bladder removed, two toes removed, a pinched nerve rerouted around his elbow. And he had also undergone hospitalization for a crushed chest suffered in a head-on collision. None of this slowed him up for long, but now, as he grew older, he lived in almost constant pain from some of these old injuries.

Sylvester, on the other hand, had reached old age with very few physical problems. He was active, could walk without pain, and continued to putter about the yard almost as well as ever.

Then Sylvester had some terrible luck. He and Mae had made it a practice in later years to spend their winters in Kansas staying with children. On one of these visits Sylvester was in a serious car accident. He survived and recovered but was never the same afterwards. Fate had done in an instant what 85 years of living had failed to do. It made him a semi invalid and undoubtedly shortened his life.

So the half-century rivalry between father and Sylvester—if it had been rivalry—was now over. Sylvester was gone, while father, both bloodied and bowed, was still on his feet but just barely. Both of these two originals, as tough and stubborn as they come, had lived a life of their own choosing beholden to none but God and family. They both achieved an advanced age and lived to enjoy the fruit of their labors. Although each marched to a totally different drummer—or thought they did—the fruit of their labors was remarkably similar. Both enjoyed a comfortable and financially secure old age on the shores of a lake where they had spent half of their lives. Both produced strong and reasonably well adjusted offspring who did not turn to crime, drink to excess, or beat their spouses. Both had grandchildren who were the delight of their old age, though Sylvester far outperformed father in this regard. Sylvester's grandchildren were sufficient in number to fill a small city, or settle a new country.

So what lessons could I draw from observing the lives of these two men? That there was more than one way to skin a cat, or raise a family? That neither had won out over the other, or lost either? And was the unspoken rivalry I thought I saw between these two men simply a product of my imagination?

One final incident did indeed make me wonder. Father had worked hard all his life and now—in his retirement—was financially independent. One of the rewards of working hard in a successful business is that you can afford material possessions beyond the reach of those living on a fixed income.

Father could afford nice cars but refused to spend his money on a new one. So for many years he drove previously owned Lincoln Town-cars which provided him with all the comfort he required. These luxury automobiles also made a statement about the value of hard work and success. Father was proud of his Lincolns.

Then one day when I was home for a weekend visit I saw a classy older car leaving Sylvester's driveway.

"Whose car is that?" I asked in all innocence.

Father was silent for a moment. He just looked at me. And then he answered in a voice heavy with disgust or perhaps weariness: "That's Sylvester's car." he said. "The old fool bought himself a Cadillac."

11

FRIENDS AND FOLLIES OF A FRESHMAN

There is hardly any way I could have been worse prepared to start college at UMD in the fall of 1957. On the day classes began I had no place to live, had not registered for any classes, had missed freshman orientation so I knew nobody, knew nothing of the layout of the campus, had no advisor, and did not know how to even begin to rectify the situation in which I found myself. On a previous Saturday I had driven to Duluth to take a writing exam, but it was only a few days before that I had received notice by mail that I had been accepted as a student. Now began a mad scramble to officially enroll.

Several times during the past two weeks I had been tempted to chuck the whole idea of submitting myself to the discipline of study after the freedom and steady paycheck of the working world. I had a very interesting job with the DNR, many good friends, and the long term value of a college education was not nearly so well documented as it is today. I suppose I was simply afraid. Would I fail? Would I fit in? At 22 I was not only older than most freshman, but as old as the graduating seniors.

On this first day of class I had left home at dawn to allow for the two-hour drive to the UMD campus. My bags were packed and in the rear seat, a sign that I was going somewhere, but where that somewhere was remained a mystery. When I arrived at the campus parking lot a few early risers were going in with their books, acting for all the world as if they knew where they were headed. How I envied them.

Despite the anxieties that now possessed me I was also tremendously excited. I was learning that being totally alone among strangers leaves you open and somewhat receptive to whatever comes along. I was, as it were, a blank slate in the unknown, unattached and uncommitted, my future in the process of being written from the beginning. In that fall day in 1957 I felt myself to be all potential, like well watered and fertile ground prepared for the planting.

I very reluctantly got out of my car that bright fall morning, found the business office, was assigned an advisor, and by the end of the day had registered for all my classes. They were not easy classes either: Freshman English, Zoology, Chemistry, Psychology. In those days students were expected to graduate in four years, so a 15-credit course load was the norm. Reviewing this list now I am somewhat surprised that I—an English major—was advised to take so many science courses. My English advisor, an ex-engineer now teaching Shakespeare, must have thought science to be good for the soul, or he wanted me to wash out as soon as possible, or—more likely—all the easy courses were filled because of my late registration.

By mid-afternoon I had paid my fees and was now officially a college student. How proud I was of this new way to define myself. In the space of a few hours I had left the teeming ranks of the illiterate and became a member of the educated elite. All without taking a single class.

I had also resolved the question of where to spend the night. A dozen miles up the shore from Duluth at French River was a State of Minnesota fish hatchery. As a long time DNR worker I had a master key which unlocked the door of every fish hatchery in the state. These hatcheries were in strategic locations: Brainerd, Detroit Lakes, Glenwood, Waterville—and each had a dormitory room with bunks to house employees traveling on state business. Over the past several years I had stayed at many of these hatcheries, including the one at French River. Because of the constant coming and going of state employees, hatchery officials were usually not particularly curious about who was staying with them at any one time. It was this lack of curiosity that I was counting on now.

Not wanting to arrive at the hatchery during working hours, and possibly be questioned about my business there. I ate a leisurely supper and arrived at the hatchery just before dark. The place was deserted. I selected a comfortable bunk and made myself at home.

It was perhaps a week before I was found out. The hatchery supervisor knew of my presence, of course, but assumed I had legitimate business there. One evening, curious about what that business might be, he paid me an unexpected visit. I had no choice but to tell him the truth—that I was a seasonal DNR employee just starting college with no place yet to live. He managed to choke off a smile, perhaps impressed with my gall, but insisted that I vacate the premises at all possible haste, or—relenting somewhat—as soon as I found another place to stay. And when I left I was to give him my precious key. It was losing my key that I regretted most.

The day after this tentative eviction the college housing office referred me to elderly widow who lived alone in a large stucco house only a few blocks from campus. For $25 a month she offered me a nice bedroom on the second floor, which included kitchen privileges and the run of the house. The widow, a Mrs. North, was a vigorous, energetic woman of 75, slightly deaf, who often cooked for me the groceries I purchased, and eventually became so possessive that she became exceeding angry if I had company over, reminding me that "I was about to spoil a good thing." Mrs. North's aging brother, who lived with us for a time, complained with some bitterness that his sister was a chronic nag who had driven her kind and gentle husband to an early death.

Despite her faults, I liked Mrs. North and much admired her musical skills. She was an accomplished pianist who had honed her talents playing in movie theaters during the days of silent films. In those days the pianist provided the film's musical score, the music played being happy, sad, or ominous depending on the scene. Mrs. North could thus produce on demand any kind of music you wanted to hear, and many evenings I sat in her darkened living room while she played for me, an audience of one. I was an appreciative audience too. Even then a Chopin melody could bring me to tears, though I had no idea what I was hearing.

On other evenings Mrs. North would invite over some musical friends from the college or the Duluth Symphony and then there would be a mini-concert in her living room with high tea afterward. On these occasions Mrs. North was proud to introduce me to her cultured friends, to prove perhaps that she had her own starving student living in her garret, which I surmised was a sort of status symbol among her wealthy peers. Still, it flattered me to be shown off, and I did my best to put on a cultured air myself, though I doubt that anyone was deceived.

Now that I had a place to live and could find my way around, I adjusted to campus life very quickly. I was still an outsider without friends, but this did not bother me at this point. For the time being, at least, I was enjoying the anonymity. Nothing was expected of me, and I could sit in the student union with a book in my lap and watch people—particularly the young co-eds—to my heart's content.

My greatest source of apprehension at this time involved my classes and impending mid-quarter exams. How much did I need to study? I had no idea. This was all new, and I did not know what to expect, or what would be required of me. It was akin to training for a race without knowing the distance.

I had a better idea of what to expect in my English Composition class because there was a paper to be written each week, but early results had not been encouraging. On my first three papers I had received an F. Fortunately, every other student in the class (around 10) had also received F grades, so I did not feel myself singled out for failure. Our instructor was a young professor in his first year of teaching and perhaps an F was his way of getting our attention. It certainly got mine. And with this professor there were many ways to earn an F. A grammatical error would do it. So would a misspelling. But what would arouse his ire the fastest was to deviate in the slightest from his assigned topic. This was a common failing of all of us. The assigned topic was often boring and it was more fun to be creative and freelance. An automatic F.

The F grades terrified me and were also inexplicable. I considered myself a good writer. People had long told me so. What was I doing wrong?

The next week I was determined to give the writing assignment everything I had—to write such a masterpiece that the professor would be forced to acknowledge my talent. I labored on this paper night after night. I had a senior honors student from my home town of McGregor read it and correct any typos or grammatical errors. The paper was perfect, the best I could do.

The day arrived for the professor to return our graded papers. I was in a state of high anticipation. Then the professor did a strange thing. Before passing out our graded papers he made an announcement. "Only two people had passing papers," he said. "One who wrote an excellent paper on the right topic. I gave that paper an A. The other person wrote a wonderful paper on the wrong topic. I should have failed that person, but I couldn't bring myself to do it. The paper was just too good." He made this announcement with an air of sadness, as though I had made him compromise his standards.

Because there was not the slightest doubt in my mind that the professor was referring to me. The returned paper confirmed it. He had given me a C, along with a written admonishment to stick to the assigned topic in the future. After so many failed papers, a C was cause for celebration, and that day marked a turning point in my writing classes. I never received another F on a paper from anyone. The secret was simple: write as well as you could, stay on topic, and—not least—type your paper. Professors claimed to judge solely on content, and perhaps they even believed this, but I never again risked submitting a handwritten paper.

The resolution of my fears in Zoology class happened in a much different way. Zoology was a five-credit course with four hours of lab work each week plus three hours of lectures. The textbook was three inches thick and full of strange Latin words. Other students shuddered when I mentioned I was taking Zoology. "It's a bear," they said. "Terribly difficult." Too late I learned that Zoology was a course that English majors avoided.

On the first day of class the Zoology professor passed out several sheets of paper containing Latin roots and their English equivalent. "Learn them," he warned. "The language of science is Latin. You can't pass this course if you don't learn the Latin."

Just as difficult were the laboratory sessions where we were required to identify preserved specimens of all the creatures we were reading about in our textbooks. I quickly learned that zoology encompasses the whole vast range of life on earth—from the tiniest virus to humankind itself. As the life forms became larger, it was not sufficient to simply identify the creature under study. In the case of frogs, lobsters and rats, one was expected to recognize and name every blood vessel, muscle, and even nerves. Soon we were dissecting out these creatures ourselves, our eyes burning from the formaldehyde in which these unfortunate beasts had been preserved. This was a required course for pre-med students. If they succeeded in their studies they would soon be dissecting cats, dogs, and finally cadavers from the local morgue.

Though difficult, Zoology was one of the most interesting and useful courses I took while at the university, and it had a profound influence on the future direction of my life. After scoring high on my first mid-quarter exam, I was offered a job as a research assistant in the Biology department. This experience in turn led to a technical writing job with Honeywell following graduation, and later to a long medical writing career with Medtronic, where an English and Zoology background was the perfect fit. This, of course, was far in the future and for now I had no destination in mind except college itself.

I wonder now if I was not particularly fortunate in the role models and mentors that crossed my path during these early college days. The professor to whom I was assigned to assist with research was a Chinese immigrant who had become an international authority on the European corn borer and other agricultural pests. Over the years he had published dozens of technical articles in prestigious scientific journals, and one could hardly read an article in his field without finding his name referenced as the original observer of various insect phenomena. I greatly admired this brilliant and gentle man who had become famous in his field despite having to write in a language not his own. He was a genius, and I was much flattered that he took the time to give me advice. "Do research and publish the results." he said. "Become expert in something. Take time to observe. Gather the data—for years if necessary. But don't think you need the whole story at once. Every important observation is worth a paper. Publish, publish. That's the secret of getting recognized."

His real secret, I suspect, was one known and practiced by innumerable immigrants before him—to work hard and not waste time. In addition to his research and writing, the good professor carried a full teaching load and always had time to talk to his students, with whom he was a great favorite. He was also a good husband and father, listening with great patience as his wife or children related the latest crisis at home. He did all this seemingly without effort, but it could not have been easy. He was simply incredibly efficient with his time, able to switch from one activity to another—from teaching to writing to research, without losing his place or the thread of his previous thoughts. He was my mentor, friend and supervisor for the next three years.

◆　　◆　　◆

Midway through my freshman year a friend and neighbor from Sandy Lake came to me with a suggestion: why not take my evening meal where he did—with a farm family from north of McGregor who were temporarily renting an apartment in Duluth so that the father of the house and their three daughters could all attend UMD. The mother of the house took in laundry, did cleaning, and cooked an evening meal for students to help pay the family's way through college. The cost of the meal was minimal—perhaps $30 a month for a well balanced evening meal, plus a noon lunch which Mrs. Booker packed the night before.

The offer seemed too good to pass up, and so it proved to be, quite aside from the meal itself. The Bookers were, without question, the most delightful family I ever encountered, and forever after they formed my ideal of what a family ought to be. They were kind, loving, devout, generous—each family member interesting in their own way. In a week they were treating me like a son and I would have been proud indeed to have been a son in this family.

Cecil—the father—was perhaps 60 when I met him and was attending UMD to obtain his four-year degree. Years earlier he had attended the University of Chicago and obtained a two-year teaching certificate. For many years he and his wife Winnie had taught at a country school north of McGregor close to the family homestead. Now, apparently, a two-year degree was no longer sufficient qualification to teach. Cecil tried retiring on the family farm but soon got bored and depressed. Now he was back in college to get his BS and resume teaching. His daughters had also reached college age, which prompted the whole family to move to Duluth where they could attend college together.

Cecil was a teacher by nature as well as by occupation. He was a soft-spoken, gentle man, tall and angular with thinning hair, who seemed to me to be the personification of the distracted scholar. I used to see him from time to time marching across the campus lawn, bent forward at the waist as though slightly off balance, taking those long woodsman strides which would have seemed more at home on a forest trail. On campus he always seemed in a hurry and a little distracted. One almost had to block his way to get his attention. In the isolation of the forest, of course, he noticed everything, but here on a crowded campus there were too many distractions, and he shut them all out as many country people do.

Cecil was insatiably curious, a self-taught naturalist who could provide you with the common and scientific names of every green plant and woody bush growing in the vicinity of his farm. I loved to follow him in his meanderings there while he named this plant and that bush, told me its life cycle, named its relatives—even took me to his secret place under the pines on a back forty where the rare and fragrant arbutus grew.

Cecil held forth in the same way at his dinner table each evening, sharing his knowledge and interests with all the students gathered there. Dinner at the Booker table was an education and a delight, as informative and interesting as any college class.

I loved Mrs. Booker (we called her Winnie) no less than Cecil. If Cecil was captain of the family ship, so to speak, Winnie was the ship itself and the wind and the North Star. It was she who—through unrelenting labor and personal sacrifice—put her entire family through college at the same time. She was the closest thing to a saint I ever met.

When I joined the Booker table for dinner Winnie was cooking for five hungry students and also packing a noon lunch for each of us. She also took in laundry and cleaned other people's homes in her free time. During the summer she returned to the family farm—often alone—to can dozens of quarts of meat and vegetables for serving to hungry students once school began.

Despite her crushing workload, Winnie was invariably cheerful and good natured. She was witty and quick, and we boys loved to tease her and have her tease us in return. She was small but solidly built, with a sweet oval face upon which weariness (or perhaps patience) sat like a crown. She wore her once black hair combed straight back, giving her a somewhat severe look, but when she smiled her face glowed with that surprising radiance one used to catch from time to time on the face of nuns before they traded in their black garb for more modish clothes.

While dinner was being served, Winnie usually stood quietly in the background, but I quickly discovered that she was literate, articulate, and a romantic. From time to time, if I coaxed her enough, she would share with me one of her favorite poems. I loved to engage her in serious conversation, and soon decided that out of a bright and talented family—she was the brightest of them all. Yet she was taking in washing and ironing so her family could move up a notch in the world. This kind of unselfish sacrifice was totally foreign to my experience; it boggled my mind and nearly made me weep. I had to believe that when she stood with her family before their Maker she herself would carry off the highest honors.

If Winnie saw herself as a martyr because of her labors I never detected it. In the time I knew her I never heard her complain or even a hint of complaint. Any suggestion that she was working too hard would be brushed off with a laugh and a change of subject. She refused to listen to that kind of talk. It was nonsense. People had their roles. You could perform that role cheerfully or with bitterness but it was still your role. To do it well brought one happiness. It was in fact the only way to happiness. Perhaps Winnie was secretly frustrated and complained to Cecil in private, but if so they concealed it well. At that age I was a master at sniffing out hypocrisy, and I found none of it in either Cecil or Winnie.

The Bookers were a devout Christian family who had taken me and my friends—young infidels all—into their home and family. When it came to religion we were skeptics at best. Cecil and Winnie would listen to our more outrageous statements with their shy smile and then overwhelm us not with argument but with their beauty of soul and transparent goodness. These were good people who never preached, but their lives and character gave the lie to our nonsense. It was there I first learned that the life of a saint is more compelling than all the learned arguments ever conceived.

Not that life had always been smooth sailing for the two elder Bookers. It seems that when Cecil and Winnie were young and dating they quarreled for some reason. Cecil left at night in a huff and did not return for six or seven years, which probably passed quickly enough for Cecil, who was living the life he loved in the Alaskan wilderness working on the Alcan Highway. How Winnie spent this long separation I was never told. But one day Cecil returned, his anger and wanderlust apparently burned away, and Winnie was there waiting. They resumed their courtship and were eventually married.

This story—told to me by a friend who had heard it from one of the Booker daughters—fired my imagination. This was the kind of love celebrated in the great novels—a tale of unswerving devotion and steadfast loyalty which had withstood the test of time and separation. What was time to people who truly loved? I had no doubt that Winnie would have waited twice as long, perhaps forever.

I am certainly romanticizing these people. Undoubtedly they had their failings, fears, and feet of clay. But I never saw it. And it was not that they were putting on a charade for my benefit. They wee humble people, without guile or pretense, and touchingly vulnerable. Their apparent vulnerability was also their shield of protection. I would rather have bitten off my tongue than speak to them an unkindness.

One afternoon on a warm spring day I returned to the Booker home for dinner after an afternoon of drinking beer with some friends. I was famished and a little drunk. Mrs. Booker had put a meatloaf on the table which was supposed to feed six of us. I helped myself first and took half of the meatloaf, Nobody said a word but I realized that a sudden silence had descended upon the table. My college friends were looking at me. I finally realized why, and returned most of the meatloaf to the serving plate. Nothing was said, but I sensed a collective sigh of relief. Dinner conversation sprang anew as though nothing had happened. Perhaps nothing had.

Those dinners at the Booker table are still vivid after more than 40 years. One of the guests at our table was a student from Norway. Another was a gay youth from somewhere out east who was taking a degree in music. This was an interesting and diverse group with Cecil usually facilitating the discussion. He had the gift of all good teachers, the ability to draw people out, to engage everyone in the conversation.

After dinner all of us students would disperse to our separate rooms. Occasionally—particularly if the Booker daughters were home for the evening—my friend Bob and I would be invited to stay for the evening. We sang songs to the accompaniment of my guitar, and Winnie taught me to play one of her old favorites, "Scarlet Ribbons," which a popular folk group was about to return to popularity. I cannot hear that song today without being swept back to the Booker living room and the good conversation, friendship, and music we shared so many years ago.

The school term ended and so did my dinners at the Booker apartment. Cecil Booker, age 60-something, graduated from college along with Susan, his oldest daughter. Two younger daughters, Sarah and Deborah, would also graduate from UMD in the next few years. Cecil took a job teaching in a one-room schoolhouse in the wilds of northern Minnesota. There were only a few students in the school, but how lucky they were to have Cecil and Winnie as their teachers. For years the two of them had taught as a team, and the student body became their new family. Some of these students, I am convinced, must have been profoundly influenced—as I was—by the Booker's instruction and example.

I saw the Bookers a few times in later years when they were home for the summer living on the family homestead and growing the large garden which would feed them during the coming school year. The Booker farm had been carved out of dense forest in a remote area just south of the present site of Savannah State Park by Winnie's ancestors. These people were literate and knowledgeable farmers who knew about such things as fertilizer and the rotation of crops. This had once been a fine farm and still was, though the fields now were used only for hay. There still remained a large barn on the property, and a solid frame house painted white which sat on a hill above the road amidst mature oak and lilacs.

My last visit to the Booker homestead remains in my mind as symbolic of all that this good family represented. One Sunday morning in late summer I stopped by their home with my wife and young children on our way to Sandy Lake. The freshly mowed lawn was bustling with people. The Booker daughters were all there with their spouses and children. There was an itinerant pastor there who Cecil had dragged home from church after the Sunday service. A table and chairs had been set up outside on the lawn and the table sagged with steaming platters of fried chicken, mashed potatoes, dressing, fresh garden vegetables, and all the trimmings. It was dinnertime. The Bookers had company and we were intruders.

I wanted to escape but too late. We had been spotted. Cecil collared us in a thrice and dragged us protesting to their already crowded table. Winnie had a smile a mile wide and the daughters greeted us with delight. We made the pastor's introduction and grace was said over the food. What joy emanated about that table! What free and spontaneous conversation! I felt like the prodigal son returning home after a long absence, except home was never like this. I felt more love and welcome here than anywhere I had ever been except perhaps at the family table of Old Jim.

This Sunday was the last time I saw the Booker family. I was now living in the twin cities and our lives had taken different directions. I thought about them many times but never got around to writing. They were as gone from my life as if swallowed by some black hole, but it was I who had disappeared. It seems incredible to me now that one could be so careless of precious friendship, as though the friend would always be there waiting when you finally decided to pay a visit.

Whether this be folly or simply a young man's fate, the poet Kingsley captures the consequences perfectly:

"When all the world is young, lad And all the trees are green, And every goose a swan, lad And every lass a queen. Then hey for boot and horse, lad, Around the world away. Young blood must have its course, lad And every dog his day.

When all the world is old, lad And all the trees are brown And all the sport is stale, lad And all the wheels run down. Creep home to take your place there, the spent and mained amoung. God grant you find one face there you loved when all was young."

Perhaps nature meant it that we each go off to our own particular war, and that it is only later—if we have the good fortune to survive—that we can reflect upon and weep for those we abandoned.

12

SOPHOMORE HI-JINKS

When I returned to college for my sophomore year I was no longer the fearful, apprehensive supplicant of the year before. Now I felt I belonged. I had friends, a campus job, knew some of my professors, and could find my way around without getting lost. Nor did I have any doubts now about doing college-level work. I had worried about this initially, perhaps because I had graduated from the tiny, backwater town of McGregor where the teachers were not always the best. However, I had been fortunate to have had very good teachers at critical times in the classes that mattered most—English, math, chemistry—and discovered that I was as well prepared for college as graduates of the larger Duluth or Minneapolis schools.

Wanting more independence, instead of renewing my lease in the home of Mrs. North, I decided to rent an upstairs apartment on East Superior street with my friend Pete from the Twin Cities, the first acquaintance I had made upon starting college the year before. Pete and I had hit it off immediately because of our shared outdoor interests, and by the end of the school year had become close friends. Pete had enrolled at UMD to play football, and had made the team, but poor grades as a result of too much partying soon made him academically ineligible.

Pete was hurt and saddened by his dismissal from the football team, and put his energies into more serious partying. He had arrived at college the year before the essence of the All American Boy—a fine athlete who neither smoked, drank, or swore—but he had embraced these vices almost at once and simultaneously. I, of course, had all of these vices already, but had been at them longer, and was still their master.

Pete, however, fell in love with the way alcohol rounded out his personality. It is safe to say that he became a heavy and serious drinker after his first drink, and he could soon polish off a fifth of bourbon in an evening setting. At the time, many of Pete's fraternity brothers drank too much, and Pete's drinking did not draw undue attention. He held his liquor well, and retained good judgment when he drank—not like some of his fraternity friends who drank to the point of temporary insanity. But there were danger signs for Pete even then. If there were no party, he would sometimes put on sad music and drink alone—a dangerous habit I thought for a sensitive, inherently melancholy person like Pete. At the time both of us were undergoing heartbreak due to the loss of our latest girlfriends, so I quite understood his unhappiness, but I had discovered for myself that drinking made me unhappier still.

Our Superior Street apartment soon became the party place for some of Pete's fraternity brothers. I had become a competent guitarist by this time and had mastered all the hit songs of the Kingston Trio who were then at the height of their popularity. Two or three nights a week we held sing-alongs in the apartment and our group of three or four people got quite good—so good that we thought we were ready for the local talent contests. These sing-alongs disturbed the other tenants in our three-story home and aroused the ire of our landlord, but we managed to avoid eviction until we made the mistake of allowing another guitarist into the group. The new guitarist was a 6' 10' football player of proportional girth who—while stomping his foot on the floor in time with the music—started the plaster falling off the ceiling in the room below, and the baby howling who dwelled therein. We were thrown out in a thrice, with orders never to return.

We moved next to a small apartment above a garage on 18th Avenue East and 2nd street where we could play our music to our heart's content. Soon there was a constant stream of revelers making their way up the stairs to our secluded apartment. Among the party goers were Pete's fraternity brothers, student nurses from St Lukes and St Marys hospitals, as well as Pete's future wife and friends of friends who had heard our apartment was the place to come for music and good conversation. Occasionally a fraternity brother would creep up our stairs late at night, often after we had gone to bed, with some lady gleaned from the streets after the bars had closed. These unexpected disturbances ruined our sleep.

Nor was there any way to sleep through the tumult. The apartment was small, consisting of two rooms—a tiny kitchen and a small living room just large enough to hold the two bunk beds in which Pete and I slept. There was only about four feet of space separating the two beds, so the late night partying usually took place with someone sitting on the edge of the bed, even while we were in it trying to sleep. One night I decided that enough was enough. Some of the people in the room I hardly knew. Roaring with anger, I lept from my bed in a simulated rage, clad only in my briefs, and chased all the revelers down the stairs. They fled the building taking two steps at a time, thinking that I must have gone berserk. We had fewer late night visitors after that, particularly strangers. Our friends were undeterred.

Some of the worst nuisances were our fraternity brothers. Our apartment had a tiny closet in which we stored a mattress from a twin bed. If a friend needed a place to spend the night, the mattress was dragged into the kitchen, the table and chairs were pushed aside, and a makeshift bedroom resulted. When the existence of this mattress became known, people began arriving late at night—not to sleep—but simply to borrow the mattress. Through a haze of sleep one would hear the closet door squeak open, a groping about in the dark for the folded mattress, a slithering as the mattress was dragged into the kitchen, the scraping of table legs on the linoleum floor, feminine giggles or protests as the case might be. Later one would hear the front door quietly close. On at least one occasion we woke up to find our mysterious visitor gone, and his lady friend still asleep in our kitchen. It was up to us to drive her home.

Despite the partying, I still managed to get some studying done during the day in the student union or in the library, but the grades of my younger friends suffered and they soon found themselves on probation. By the end of winter quarter they had dropped out of school and headed for the beaches of Florida without so much as a dollar between them.

Just up the street from our apartment was a tiny grocery store owned by a Jew who was perhaps in his mid fifties. One day my roommate and his buddy walked up to the little store and attempted to steal a frozen chicken. The owner spotted the boys in the act of theft, came out from behind the counter, retrieved the filched chicken from under my friend's trench coat, and returned the chicken to his freezer. "If you fellows are hungry," the grocer said. "You don't have to steal. I'll put your food on a tab and you can pay me when you have money."

This story of the Jewish grocer's kindness so impressed me that I began to do all my meager grocery shopping at his store and we soon became good friends. On my wedding day several months later he offered his best wishes and a bottle of his finest wine.

The aborted chicken theft did not cure my friend (who I shall call Mike) from shoplifting. Mike was a bold and accomplished thief, and soon our unfurnished apartment was awash with pilfered items—highway signs of every description, statues and props from the stage of the campus theater, phonograph records by the dozens—finally, a console stereo he somehow managed to smuggle out of a Daytons warehouse during a short-term employment there. He was caught in the act of theft once again when recognized by a former schoolmate while fleeing from the lobby of St Mary's hospital with a two-foot-tall ashtray under his arm. Somehow he managed to convince the police that this was simply a hazing prank forced on him by his fraternity, and he escaped with no more than a warning and an apology to the irate nuns to whom the ashtray belonged.

Mike was one of those high-spirited, charming rogues who it was delightful (though somewhat dangerous) to be around. He was a risk taker—always seeking a new thrill—as well as a schemer, a shameless flatterer, and a consummate liar. One night in a nightclub he convinced some attractive young lady that I was the son of some fabulously wealthy Duluth mining baron. The young lady was ready to elope with me on the spot, but her ardor cooled when she discovered my wealth was simply a creation of Mike's vivid imagination.

Mike finally got his comeuppance when he met a young lady who was just as persuasive as he was. They conned and flattered each other something fierce, both pretending to be something more than they were. What followed was a lightning courtship and marriage before either discovered the truth. Both were good and decent people, and the truth was not all that bad, but both were somehow expecting more. At the time I considered their successful con of each other poetic justice, but I liked them both very much and was later saddened by their mutual disillusionment.

The start of their marriage was not auspicious. One evening about six Mike called from Minneapolis and asked me to find him a Justice of Peace(JP). He intended to get married that very night, and would be arriving with his prospective bride in about three hours. Despite the short notice, I found a willing J.P. living in a rural area north of Duluth, but the good man had gone to bed before the wedding pair arrived. We rousted him from bed finally after repeated banging on his door. A light popped on inside and he let us in, somewhat reluctantly, a sad sight indeed. Half asleep, his wrinkled face grizzled from a three-day growth of beard, he made ready to marry the happy couple clad only in trousers and his underwear top, from which a few scraggly grey hairs protruded from around the buttons on his chest. Behind him in the dim light a week's worth of dirty dishes filled the sink and spilled over onto the countertop, creating the impression of vile gifts carelessly opened. While he read the sacred words, a large moth fluttered about his head in erratic circles, which the poor man's bleary eyes followed against his will, as did mine and those of the wedding couple. As the moth dipped and darted abut the J.P.'s head I had to literally choke to avoid exploding in a screech of laughter. The rattled J.P.—his eyes unable to follow the moth and the text at the same time—stumbled over the words, hemmed and hawed, half gagged, and finally finished—just in time too because I was near the point of collapse.

In the car afterwards Mike and I roared with glee and did funny imitations of the J.P.'s delivery and mannerisms all the way back to Duluth. But the bride was silent and I could understand why. Her wedding day—the day of her dreams for which she had long planned—had turned instead into something bizarre, grotesque, and a travesty. This day marked the end of her youth, and of her innocence. A day or two earlier she had discovered that she was pregnant, and life for her would never be the same. The young lady came from a proud and socially prominent family. Both she and her mother had been planning a large and dignified wedding…and now this. What scandal would this create among her closely knit relatives in the small city from which she came?

Oh, she talked briefly of having her large wedding anyway, keeping this elopement a secret. The elopement would be a trump card she could play later, if necessary, to those who counted months and decided that the baby had come far too early. But this elopement, I thought, would not satisfy the gossipers. Instead of proving that she had been legally married when she became pregnant, the elopement proved precisely the opposite.

As I recall, the young couple did have their expensive wedding with over a hundred guests and scores of gifts. But it was a fraud in a sense and everyone must have soon known it. The bride's mother never forgave Mike for shaming her daughter before the town. He might have redeemed himself in time, but his was a personality that invariably found itself in ever deeper entanglements.

In those days—the waning hours of the 1950's—a great many young couples were forced into marriage because of inadvertent pregnancy. The sexual emancipation of women was beginning, but the pill—which was to prevent so many future pregnancies—had not yet arrived. The "shotgun" wedding suddenly seemed to become the norm as bungling and largely naive young couples found themselves with a child on the way.

These marriages—though forced in a sense—were probably as happy and enduring as any other. But a high price was initially paid in terms of shock, shame and pain. The unfortunately pregnant young lady still had a conscience, and her parents could still feel shame. The lady was often tormented by doubts as to whether her new husband really loved her, or whether he married her only because he "had to." The young man, so recently flushed with the thrill of seduction, and probably praised by his buddies for his "way with a maid," now sobered up in a hurry and saw stretching before him an unrelenting future and the heavy arm of responsibility. For both young people, carefree youth had vanished as suddenly as a thunderclap.

Such may have been the thoughts of the newlyweds as we drove back to Duluth that evening. My new wife and I dropped them at their car and watched them drive off into the night to some kind of honeymoon. But their honeymoon was over and I suspect they both knew it. The dissolution of their marriage took another 20 years, but I am convinced that the dissolution began that night in a cluttered dining room while a moth fluttered about our heads like a bad omen.

◆   ◆   ◆

Not all of our fraternity parties were unproductive. One such party on the sand beaches of Duluth's Park Point quite unexpectedly gave me a career and largely determined the future course of my life.

Like many college students I had no definite idea of what I wanted to do with my life. I knew that I was reasonably intelligent and could probably master almost any profession if I put my mind to it. But no profession particularly appealed to me. I was unmotivated and lazy too.

Some careers—like law or medicine—seemed to require too much dedication. Chemistry seemed boring. I enjoyed biology but the profession at that time did not pay well, and my college job, which involved observing and recording the flight habits of the fruit fly, would quite likely drive me to drink. Quite simply, I wanted a profession that did not interfere with my hobbies.

The only profession that seemed to meet all of my criteria was to become a writer like Hemingway which would allow me to live anywhere, indulge my hobbies, and work when I felt like it. I had learned also that I found great personal satisfaction in writing something good, and I wanted praise for my wit and insight—which occasionally happened when a professor liked something I had written. But I also realized that this dream of being a rich and successful writer was not very realistic. I might have some talent as a writer but who was willing to pay me for it? Almost everybody considered themselves a writer. They were a dime a dozen.

Then one day in one of those instances of serendipity, or fate, or chance, or the work of one's guardian angel—I happened to be attending a July 4th keg party on the beach of Park Point with some fraternity friends. I don't remember why I was attending this particular party. Ordinarily I returned to Sandy Lake on weekends. But here I was, lying on the sand drinking beer, the water of Lake Superior far too cold to swim in, though our lady hostess who owned a home on the beach was indeed swimming, either to impress us wimpy young men or because she had truly adapted to the frigid water.

I remembered lying in the sand with my beer, bored and only half listening to a popular fraternity man holding court with a small circle of admirers. This fellow was a senior English major who had already acquired a reputation as a very talented writer and something of a wit. In fact, he was already employed part time as a writer at a Duluth publishing company. Naturally I was jealous of his success and the adulation he was receiving from his friends. I simply considered him a braggart and tuned him out where possible, but now—being slightly drunk—he was talking too loud not to hear him.

Then he said something that caught my attention. "Technical writing," he said, "is the only kind of writing that pays any money." That was all I heard before he moved to another subject. But that was enough. That short sentence lit up my soul like revelation. Those words were specifically for me. This near stranger, who I did not like, had come this day to deliver those words, and I had come to receive them. In that instant I was certain of one thing. I was going to be a technical writer. I had no idea what one did, or who hired them, or what training I needed to become one. But that did not concern me. I had found my future. I now had a career.

During the next few weeks I learned a little more about what a technical writer did, but not very much. UMD had no curricula for technical writing—not even a class on the subject. My English professors had heard of it, but little more.

During my first two years of college my major had bounced back and forth between English and Biology. I had enrolled as an English major, but then switched to biology after being offered a job in the biology department. Now I was ready to switch my major back to English. I contacted my former advisor in the English department and told him my plans—that I wanted to become a technical writer and switch my major once again to English.

To my surprise, he advised against switching majors. "If you want to be a technical writer," he said. "Stay with a science major. To write abut science, you need to be technically competent in science. A science major will serve you better."

This professor of English had a rather unique background. He had trained and worked as an engineer, but then—perhaps due to a midlife crisis—decided that he would rather be teaching Shakespeare, so he returned to college and acquired a PhD in English. Here then was the right person to advise me—a technical person who was also an English major. Nevertheless, I ignored his advice and switched my major to

English. It seemed to me that I needed to become a better writer and that I would only get the necessary practice in the English department. To my way of thinking, if I learned to write well I could always learn the scientific subject matter. I also believed that one acquired a broader and better education as a liberal arts major. A science major required early specialization, and seemed to me too narrow in scope. Literature and philosophy I found far more interesting and more useful too. Interestingly, medical schools in later years came to the same conclusion, and preferred their candidates to have a liberal arts background.

Fortunately for me, my early college courses and work with the DNR as a biologist aide had given me an excellent grounding in science, and I graduated with a major in English and a minor in zoology, which everyone thought was a strange combination indeed. Years later, when I joined infant Medtronic as a medical writer, this background proved to be a near perfect fit.

That Park Point keg party and subsequent decision to become something called a "technical writer" paid off at graduation time. I received simultaneous job offers from two of Minnesota's most respected companies within three weeks of graduation.

In later years the University of Minnesota and other major schools established degree programs in technical writing. Because of my job as head of the technical writing department at Medtronic I had the privilege of consulting with the University of Minnesota when it established its technical writing curriculum. It is a curriculum quite similar to the one I had laid out for myself at UMD many years before.

13

A STUDENT'S SEARCH FOR MEANING

My three years as a research assistant in the UMD Biology department put me in the center of the ongoing debate between science and religion over the origins of life. Zoology itself was an attempt to connect the dots between lower and higher life forms, and to classify these life forms into ever smaller divisions, of which Kingdom was the broadest category and Species the narrowest. Darwin proved beyond question that a species can evolve and adapt to a particular environmental niche, One needs only to look at the many breeds of dogs to realize that the gene pool of a species is almost infinitely variable, A dog breeder with enough time might create a terrier, or a St Bernard, but there is no evidence that a dog can be turned into a cat. The scientist, of course, argues that over eons of time the primordial gene pool can produce a dog, a cat, or even man and woman.

As a young biology student I had no difficulty accepting such a concept, It seemed logical, and I had no strong religious convictions to get in the way. My love of science was not of recent origin either. It dated back to a fourth grade reader which gave me my first glimpse of the dinosaurs, and an artist's conception of our solar system. How excited I was by these new and mysterious concepts. How hungry I was to know more. To know everything.

But alas. I quickly discovered that the questions to which I wanted answers were all (and remain) unanswerable. Where did we come from? Where were we going? Why were we here? Science and religion each had their own answers, neither of which I found convincing. I wanted to believe that God was in His heaven and all was right with the world, but evidence did not seem to support it. Too many bad things happened. God did not seem to be watching over us at all, or simply did not care, which amounted to the same thing. One could conclude quite easily that human existence was simply one of God's experiments, like the dinosaurs, and that one day He might lose interest and move on to something else. Or perhaps He simply set up the experiment and watched without interfering, waiting to see how the whole thing turned out. Everyone harped abut the sanctity of life—how sacred it was—but personal observation made me question whether life was really sacred to God. He seemed quite willing to let life squander itself in bloody and apparently pointless wars. Every life form was simply food for some other life form. Tigers eating man and man eating every other species right down the line. Obviously, life had no value to God, beyond being grist for whatever experiment He had going at the time. Was God's purpose in creating the dinosaurs and the ancient forests simply to fertilize the soil and make coal and oil? It seemed possible.

If one concluded that God was uncaring or callous or simply curious, then it might be more understandable to eliminate the idea of God altogether. If life and the universe had somehow evolved on its own then God was unnecessary. Man himself was the measure of all things. Through reason, man could perfect himself and eventually create a perfect world.

College put me in the middle of the above debates and also gave me access to every argument ever written on the subject by both churchmen and secular philosophers. Religion and philosophy now became the burning interests of my life and I spent all my spare hours in the library reading upon these subjects, as well as taking every philosophy course offered by the college.

The above debate really started with the publication of Darwin's Origin of Species in the late 19th century and had been raging ever since. Neither side, in my opinion, could make a wholly convincing argument for their point of view. The evolutionists argued that the universe did not need God to explain its beginnings or the arrival of life on earth. The church people based their beliefs on scripture, but biblical science was faulty and cast doubt on the whole. The philosophers based their arguments both for and against the existence of God using analogies: The universe was a clock winding down, therefore someone (God) must have wound it up initially. Like the watchmaker, He then stepped out of the picture. Evolution was a logical explanation up to a point, but it could not explain man's moral nature—his conscience, or willingness to die for a friend or a belief. The religious martyrs who went to the stake rather than recant their faith—what power impelled them? Why had the message of Christ survived for 2000 years—continually renewing itself—despite all the attempts by kings and philosophers to stamp it out my means of the rope, fire, or ridicule?

The above agonizings may have proved pointless, but they were not unimportant. This was not simply an academic debate. On the contrary, the way a person answered these questions had a profound impact on how you chose to live your life. It could mean the difference between happiness and despair, peace of mind, or permanent anxieties, phobias—even suicide. And not only was your own peace of mind at stake here, but perhaps the future happiness of your children.

After all my reading and pondering I found myself just where I started. There were no absolute answers but there was a simple conclusion: one either believed in God on one did not. Either viewpoint had to be taken on faith. The atheist was as much a True Believer as the religious fanatic.

Without any satisfaction or serious answers forthcoming, I turned then to that great debunker of the 1920's, H.L. Mencken, who wrote wonderfully witty and sarcastic attacks on every institution in American life. God, mom, apple pie, democracy, religion—he spared none of them. He wrote of Baptists leaping from their graves into interstellar space with roars of joy, wings sprouting from their scapulae. All of this seemed wonderfully funny to me, and Mencken had me literally rolling on the floor. If I could not understand life, I could at least laugh at it, and I introduced Mencken—who had been dead and long forgotten—to other like-minded friends in the Biology department. Mencken's writings became our bible and he our prophet—the only writer we knew who had the courage to deflate our pretensions and society's most sacred beliefs.

What was a little sobering perhaps was that Mencken had spent the last eight years of his life in a chair, fully alert but unable to speak, write, or communicate in any way—the result of a stroke that felled him in the prime of life. Had he suffered the wrath of God? I did not rule it out. If any man deserved to be silenced for a mocking spirit and blasphemy it was Mencken. My friends and I were not particularly concerned about this at the time. We were young, and there seemed to be plenty of time ahead to repent and let God know that…hey, we were only kidding.

I discovered before much time passed that the wit of a skeptic is no more substantial than the mutterings of a fool in the wind. Tolstoy in Anna Karenina likened the man without faith to one standing shivering in the cold in a cheap muslin garment. The gift of faith on the other hand was like being suddenly handed a warm fur coat—the difference literally between life and death.

I learned first hand just how bankrupt my philosophy was when my young wife's mother died of cancer, and my brother-in law Terry and I volunteered to dig her grave. It was a fool's task, I suppose, performed by fools, but it seemed at the time a way for the two of us to save a poor widower some funeral expenses.

Terry and I were standing in the widower's yard making our plans in a whisper so the grieving widower would not know what we were up to. We needed another shovel and did not know where to find one. Neither did my wife's younger sisters who were still living at home.

Just as we were about to start a search, the widower suddenly appeared from the direction of the barn carrying a shovel. He had apparently overheard us talking. Without saying a word, he handed me the shovel and returned to the house.

There was something about that act of handing me the shovel that drove home—more than anything else had ever done—the finality and banality of death, and something about courage too. The shovel was a symbol, and not one I liked. Was digging the grave of a young mother no different than burying the carcass of a dog? The same shovel would do for both. How did one reconcile this terrible thought? That we were no different than the beasts?

I wrestled with these questions for all of my 20's and most of my 30's. I wanted to believe that life had meaning and purpose but was unable to do so. People of faith I feared were ignorant or deluded. I suspected that Marx had it right: that religion was simply the "opiate of the people.," a useful tool to keep society from flying apart.

And then one day to my great surprise I was unexpectedly handed that warm fur coat of which Tolstoy had written. From that day on life took on—not new meaning—but meaning period. I literally wept for joy.

But that momentous event was still far in the future, and in the meantime I was destined to remain shivering in the muslin rags of the skeptic.

14

WEDDING BELLS

I met my future wife Katherine in the middle of my freshman year at a dance pavilion on Sandy Lake. She had arrived with her steady boyfriend and I was alone. The boyfriend left her unattended for a moment while he went in search of the restroom, and in his absence I asked her to dance. The dance was an old time waltz and we danced until the music changed. I suppose we talked but I do not remember what was said.

When I returned Katherine to her boyfriend he was fuming. He grabbed her coat and hustled her out the door without a word of explanation. The girl went home that night and told her mother that she had found the man she was going to marry. Being unaware of this presumptuous decision, I went on with my life quite undisturbed.

I saw her again the next fall at a football game in McGregor where she was attending high school. Sometime during the game I managed to wedge my way in beside her and remain there. Eventually we struck up a conversation. I was not sure if she remembered dancing with me nearly a year before, and did not mention it. She, of course, remembered it very well. After all, I was the man she was going to marry.

As we parted I suggested paying her a visit one day. After all, we were practically neighbors. She smiled and did not say no. I was serious about another girl at the time and little thought anything would result from this chance meeting. Still, I was very much attracted to this beautiful young woman, and, one never knew…

How right I was. That winter, my serious girlfriend, with whom I had been carrying on a long distance courtship through letters and weekend visits—suddenly dumped me without warning. No explanation was forthcoming. It was simply over, she said. Don't come. Don't call. I won't be available.

This occurred just before Christmas. I was stunned and dumbfounded. This could not be happening. Happiness could not end like this—like a bolt from the blue or the wrath of an angry God. I did in fact believe that it was the wrath of God. I was being punished for past sins, some recent.

I remember, a few nights later, riding to midnight mass with Old Jim and his family. It was very cold, every star in the sky ablaze, and I was alone and heartbroken in an infinite, empty universe. I was quite certain that I would never be happy again.

Spring finally came, and more and more often I thought of that lovely farm girl who I had promised one day to visit. One day in March I decided to put that promise into action. My friend Eddy knew the young lady better than I and also knew where she lived. I commissioned him to go to the door and invite the lady outside, at which point I would invite her for a Sunday drive.

Instead of following instructions, Eddie asked the young lady to go riding with him, and I suffered the indignity of driving the two of them around all afternoon while they spooned away in the back seat. I was angry and jealous but knew it was my own fault. Never send a man to do a boy's job.

The young lady had to be home in time for evening chores so this painful episode finally ended. After we returned to her home she invited me in to play my guitar, which I always carried with me in anticipation of just such an opportunity. My guitar had opened many doors for me in the past and I was reasonably confident that it could undo the mess that young Eddie had made of the afternoon. Eddie might look like young Robert Redford, but he could not play the guitar.

I carried my guitar into the tiny living room and found a chair. The girl Katherine and her three younger sisters crowded onto a nearby couch, her mother standing in the background, non-committal, as though trying to decide whether to let me stay or throw me out. The father of the family, who Kathy mentioned also played the guitar, was in bed with pneumonia. I could hear him coughing in a back bedroom. All the girls were waiting in silence, hands in their laps and an expectant look on their faces, the whole setting reminiscent of a drawing room scene from Jane Austin's Sense and Sensibility.

I played and sang a few of the popular country songs of the day and then sang a fast-paced novelty tune to Katherine's young sister who was perhaps seven or eight years old. The song was a hit with the little girl and it brought the father of the house out of his sickroom. So weak he could hardly stand, his hands trembling, he emerged from his bedroom with his own guitar and we played a few songs together. He attempted to sing also, for he was a fine singer, but tonight his voice was hoarse and wracked by fits of coughing. But I could tell that the girl Katherine was pleased by all this. I had passed a test of some sort; her parents liked me. From time to time when I shot her a glance she slipped me a shy smile that I could interpret as I would. From what I could see those smiles were for me rather than Eddie. I drove home that evening in a state of euphoria, hardly remembering to chide Eddie for his earlier treachery in making a play for the young lady I wanted for myself.

The following Sunday when I visited her home once again I left Eddie behind and did my own asking. The young lady accepted and after that I was at her home nearly every weekend. In my pursuit of Katherine I did not neglect the rest of the family either. I brought along my work clothes, helped clean the barn, pitch down hay, and was soon milking the three cows that her mother ordinarily milked. I also found time to play guitars with her father, and banter with her younger sisters.

At the end of May Katherine graduated from high school. I attended the event with her parents and sisters like another member of the family. The following Monday she was due to start work at St Lukes hospital in Duluth as a nursing trainee.

On the Thursday before she was to begin work, I picked up Katherine at her farm place and moved her to the YWCA in Duluth where she would be living while going through nurses training. She was easy to move, owning nothing but an old suitcase and perhaps a dress or two. Were there tears and grief as the first daughter left home to an unknown future? In my own selfishness I do not remember. Her three young sisters were pensive and quiet, her parents undemonstrative. Katherine's father was perhaps closest to weeping as he hugged Katherine goodbye. She had been his hunting partner, his confidante, his son—and he would probably miss her the most.

But any gloom we might have felt soon lifted. Leaving home for Katherine—as it had been for myself—was equivalent to being freed from jail. She was a song bird let out of the cage, and our joy knew no bounds.

The next day Katherine and I traveled up the North Shore to spend the weekend with a family in Grand Marais. This was our first trip together, and set the pattern for many trips to come. It was June, sunny and warm, and we were in love. Not a sparkling brook, a waterfall, a cliff, or a hiking trail did we allow to pass unexamined as we made our way north. Splitrock lighthouse, Silver Cliff, The Palisades, Castle Danger, Manitou Falls—the very names were cloaked in romance and mystery. We discovered that day that we shared an insatiable curiosity to see what was beyond the hill, around the next bend, in the mist across the river. This first trip together up the North Shore was one of those peak experiences one always remembers. In years to come there would be many more: our first sight of the Bighorns, the Lake Solitude hike in the Tetons, our first drive up the Beartooth Pass and Going to the Sun Road, the Olympic Mountains, riding in a horse-drawn carriage through the Canadian city of Victoria. So many adventures to come, yet none more exciting than to be young and in love on a June day on the windswept shores of Gitche Gumi.

We were married that August. Just prior to the wedding we had rented a one-room apartment in an old house on fourth street, just up the hill from St Lukes Hospital. From there Katherine could easily walk to work while I used our one old car for driving to school. Our new living quarters were also on the bus line so I could catch the bus to school should that be necessary. Our rent was $25 a month, everything included.

We were very pleased with our little apartment. It was a single room, about the size of an average bedroom, with an adjoining kitchenette built into what had once been a pantry. The kitchenette held a few tiny cupboards, painted white, and a sink and a stove, between which only one person could pass at a time. Above the sink was a window which looked out on the side of a neighboring house. A single upstairs bathroom served the entire household, which included not just us, but another apartment in addition to the extended family of our landlady.

The owner of the home was an elderly widow, thin as a rail but of active disposition, forever talking and always working. She gave the impression of being both wise and cunning, intensely proud of her ability to support herself, and thus opinionated and free with advice. There was no civic, political, or moral question that she lacked an answer for. In addition to two rental rooms, the old lady was providing living quarters to a married daughter in her forties, her lazy husband, and their two children, the oldest fourteen and the youngest perhaps five.

Our landlady was raising these two grandchildren while their parents seldom left their room or removed themselves from bed for days on end. I never quite understood the arrangement. Perhaps the husband worked nights and slept all day. At any rate the wife stayed in bed also and left the housework and child raising to her aging mother. As one passed their room on the way to the bathroom you could see their shadowy forms lying in the darkness through their open door and the stale smell of sweat and dirty bed linens wafting into the hall. The room was a veritable pigsty and the occupants suited the room perfectly. Both daughter and the husband had the vacant look of the truly stupid.

These sleepy parents, as I mentioned, had a 14 year old daughter who ran wild and was already out of control when Kathy and I moved in. This girl was tall for her age and well developed, could pass for 18 and often did, and had a hankering for men far too old for her. Every few weeks she would run away from home, the police would be sent to find her, and she would invariably be found with some older man who would invariably be hauled off to jail for contributing to the girl's delinquency, though I am sure she was far past the point where any further contributions were needed.

The poor girl had no chance, I suppose, being ignored by her parents and spoiled by her grandmother, but she was truly a bad apple whose language to her parents and grandmother would shame a sailor. Any challenge to the girl's will would provoke a stream of obscenities which continued unabated until she ran out of breath, or until the hapless victims removed themselves from her presence.

Katherine and the granddaughter were on friendly terms for the first few months of our stay in this strangely dysfunctional household. Then one day the young lady stole some of Katherine's clothes and the battle was on.

At the time we moved in there was a young couple renting the room adjoining ours. The husband was a mechanic at some local garage and the wife remained home all day. Both husband and wife were quiet and soft spoken. But we soon discovered that their polite demeanor was covering a violent side, perhaps on the part of both parties. They fought incessantly, every night, their verbal battles escalating until one could hear—through the plaster walls—a sudden ominous silence, followed by the thump of blows being struck, the smack of a clenched fist, muffled grunts, howls of enraged pain from one or both of the battlers.

As time went on these daily battles increased in fury. Their verbal abuse expanded in volume and in imaginative language; there was the sound of objects being thrown, perhaps knives, and threats on both sides to murder the other. Katherine and I both feared that it was only a matter of time until one or the other pulled a gun and began shooting, the walls of our tiny room offering scant protection should we be in their line of fire.

Fortunately, before this happened, our landlady threw them out, which demonstrates how dangerous this young couple had become, for our landlady was tolerant to the extreme and already had a houseful of crazy people.

We were delighted when our feuding neighbors moved, for we inherited their much larger and nicer apartment which, at one time, had been the home's living room. Its walls were paneled with oak and there were many built-in cabinets with glass doors which gave the room a warm and cheerful aspect. Our rent increased to $35 a month.

But now we had room for a Christmas tree, and space in one corner for a platform rocker where I could study in the evenings and where later Katherine would rock our new baby. The kitchenette, once again, had been levered into a walk-in pantry, but we now considered ourselves basking in luxury.

As before, the room had a single twin bed in one corner, and when father saw our sleeping arrangements he muttered to mother: "Katherine will be pregnant all the time." And so she was. Before we left this apartment we had one child and another on the way.

Our son Donald was born the following spring. On a Monday morning, after spending the weekend with my parents on Sandy Lake, we returned to Duluth so I could attend my late morning classes at the college. Katherine was feeling poorly and went straight to bed. When I returned from school around 4:30, Katherine got out of bed where she had spent the day and her uterine water broke. This was apparently an urgent sign that the baby was on its way, ready or not. "Take me to the hospital," Katherine said. "And hurry." Instead of hurrying I pottered about, making myself a pot of coffee while Katherine grew increasingly impatient. But I saw no particular reason to rush. After all, there were hours of labor ahead, or so I believed. I searched for a good book to read while waiting.

The coffee was ready finally and we prepared to leave. Our destination was not St Lukes, where Katherine worked, but St Marys, where Katherine's doctor typically sent his patients. St Marys was somewhat farther away, but still no more than a ten minute drive.

I parked the car and we mounted the wide stairway leading to the entrance of St Marys. There was a wide brick patio before the entrance and I remember pausing there and looking off across the Duluth harbor half in shock, as though this peek was my last look at the familiar, unconfined world. I noticed that Katherine's lower lip was quivering. She was still a child, hardly more than 18. That quivering lip broke my heart. I took her hand and made some bumbling attempt at reassurance, but this moment was beyond words. We were both entering unknown territory, each of us going alone to our own place.

An hour later Katherine's doctor greeted me in the waiting room with a broad smile on his face. I was the father of a fine son and the mother was doing well. But the doctor waxed enthusiastic for other, more technical reasons. Never, the doctor said, had he seen a patient better suited to having children. What hips! What a magnificent pelvis! What strong abdominal muscles! He had never witnessed an easier delivery. She ought to have a dozen children!

I was not nearly as enthused as the doctor. A college classmate from McGregor happened to be the doctor's live-in nanny. I therefore knew the doctor to be a good Catholic with six children of his own. The idea of following his example made me shudder, but his prognostication proved to be true. Katherine did have six children. She not only delivered them easily, but conceived them readily regardless of what form of birth control we practiced. The doctor was right. She was made to have children.

Hardly any human experience can compare with taking home, for the first time, a child of your own—a love child, the unanticipated consequences of your months of joy and intimacy. What a responsibility a child is, and how little we considered this tiny bundle of life a responsibility! This baby was a surprise, a source of pride, something we now owned, a toy for our pleasure unlike any toy we had ever known before. Even then we were convinced that we knew enough to do the job perfectly. How wonderful is the blissful ignorance and confidence of the inexperienced.

I thought I knew from my own experience what a growing child needed. It needed love, and it needed discipline, and it needed protection—all of which we could provide despite having very little money.

And we did not consider ourselves poor in any real sense. There were in fact many times in later years when I was earning a good salary when I felt ourselves to be—and truly were—much poorer.

But in this year of our Lord 1959, I was a junior in college with a wife, a child, and yet another child on the way—without any debt, with a free heart not yet in bondage to material possessions, neither yet in bondage to the desire to be a "success," and the pressure that entails. Nobody, to my knowledge, expected anything of us, including our parents who hoped only that one day I would show some ambition and get a real job.

But we already had all the essentials: a roof over our head that we could afford, a car that was paid for, a campus job that paid for books, tuition, and living expenses. Katherine's nursing job at the hospital could be arranged around my schedule, so no day care was required. There was enough cash to buy gas for the car and shotgun shells, which kept us in fresh meat in season. We ate ducks, deer, rabbits, grouse, and one year devoured a bear. Obtaining wild game for the table provided us with both food and recreation. And if we were strapped for cash and needed adventure, there were the fascinating rivers of the nearby North Shore to explore. This was, without question, the very best of times.

0-595-22529-2

Made in the USA
Coppell, TX
26 May 2020